The Wild Thyme
Cookbook

The Wild Thyme Cookbook

Jenny Horton

BRAMBLEWOOD
PUBLISHING

Bramblewood Publishing
3, Bramblewood Close
Overton-on-Dee, North Wales, LL13 0HJ

Email: Bramblewoodpublishing@outlook.com

First published by Bramblewood Publishing, 2020
First edition: October 15th, 2020

ISBN: 978-0-9954996-2-1

Designed and typeset by Robert Davies
Scans and enhancement by Fred Langford Edwards

Printed and bound in Great Britain

Watercolour painting on front cover by Ekaterina Mikheeva
Cover design by Robert Davies

To Stuart
and Michael, Katy and Orlando,
Atticus, Angelo, Lysander and Xavier

With Love

Acknowledgements

I am much indebted to my editor **Robert Davies**, not just for his expert guidance but his abundance of the saintly qualities needed to get a book like mine off the ground: patience, generosity, good humour and more patience. It has been a real pleasure to work with him.

Secondly, thanks go to **Fred Langford Edwards** for his expert and loving 'treatment' of the old family photos. Again I found not just a professional but a great human being who is at present engaged on compiling a photographic record of the lives of the indigenous people in the Amazon jungle.

Simon Glantz, nutritionist and family friend since my children's school days, has been my mentor. His guidance on the benefits of pure food instead of processed was not only invaluable to my health but also kick-started this book.

My sister **Edna** and brother **George** have always given me constant encouragement and support for which I am so grateful. I particularly hope Edna considers this book some reward for keeping me in library books even before I could walk.

Finally, all love and gratitude goes to my husband **Stuart** without whom all the best things in my life would never have happened.

Jenny Horton qualified at Battersea College of Education in 1970 and taught for seven years before taking time out to raise a family. A growing passion for English literature resulted in a B.A. in 1985 and an M.A. in 1996. Her forty years in education happily concluded with six years as an Open University Arts lecturer.

She shares a love of nature with husband Stuart with whom she explores the wild countryside of North Wales. Live music especially folk, blues and jazz is another shared interest both as listeners and performers. Whilst Jenny is still devoted to cooking, Stuart is not. To her delight he sings for his supper instead.

Contents

Preface

TAKE medicinal drugs or adapt your diet! This is the dilemma I once faced when working on the computer all day played havoc with my joints. I chose the latter. The diet meant abandoning processed foods in favour of fresh, natural ones.

At first I panicked and bought all foods green and leafy from the supermarket and when a friend popped in, we laughed at how the kitchen looked like a grocer's shop. The air was full of floating bits of leaves and onion skins with little me in the middle, peeling, shredding and chopping away.

That approach didn't last. Instead I spent the next two years researching how to replace the processed parts of the recipes I loved with natural plant foods.

Soon I was making 'naughty' dishes with healthy, nutritious ingredients: vegetables instead of flour to thicken sauces; beetroot in chocolate cake, avocados in mousse, nut bases in tarts and nobody could spot the difference.

I catalogued the recipes for my own convenience but a friend suggested others might also be interested. And if you can have your cake and eat it, why wouldn't you?

Introduction

THIS is a very personal cookbook. Not the sort you see every day, and it is written by a Home Economist not a master chef. Home Economics embraces nutrition, aesthetics, home management and ergonomics, bringing a scientific analysis to domestic chores or pleasures, depending on how you see them. It helps you analyse how to get the best cuisine in return for the time, money and energy you spend in the kitchen.

My recipes make economical, healthy, tasty and nutritious dishes which don't exhaust the cook or our planet. Quite frankly, I always want to escape the kitchen whenever there is laughter in the lounge or sunshine outside.

A big influence has been my family. They pop up everywhere – especially in the many introductory anecdotes to each chapter. I hope you enjoy meeting them. Big sister Edna is responsible for my literary interest, having taken it on herself to keep me in library books throughout my childhood. Leaving home for London at nineteen when I was eight, she often returned with inspiring recipes and ideas about life. I was enthralled by her.

Brother George was a closer and more constant childhood companion. His forays into the countryside opened my eyes to the beauty of nature and the possibilities of eating its bounty in the form of fruit, fish and wild game. I would advise anyone coming into this world to have a big sister and brother.

But Home Economics was the greatest influence. Day-dreaming and indolence at Sale Grammar, Manchester, led me at sixteen to the Domestic Science room at the far end of the school, hidden away from academia. It housed twelve mini-kitchens, each more spacious than ours at home and in the corner, a small library of glossy cookbooks to drool over. We could cook whatever we liked in answer to assignments like: *Your brother has been at scout camp. Plan and prepare a welcome-home three-course dinner for him and the family.* (It was the 1950s.)

These cookbooks were a revelation, with recipes combining meat and fruit or pancakes that were savoury as well as sweet, vegetables stuffed with rice, herbs and nuts, fresh pears and peaches for poaching, party food like angels or devils on horseback and princely potatoes called Duchesse or Dauphinoise.

This was just scraping the surface. I was hungry for more and started collecting recipes with gusto. Before the first term was out in Lower Sixth Remove, every girl was applying for college so I did. "Don't bother with Battersea College," my Domestic Science teacher said, "It's the best and hardest to enter." Just the push I needed.

Fast forward to 1967. The Beatles reign supreme, flower power is emerging, London is swinging and I'm on a bus to Battersea College from my grand halls of residence in Queens Gate Gardens, South Kensington. Battersea was tough. The cookery classes were literally a baptism of fire but before the term was out I realised that producing tempting edible food as opposed to burnt offerings was not a matter of luck.

Everything had to be well prepared, especially your mind to know exactly what you were doing and how long it would take. It was a crash class in discipline and organization given by the most exacting and imposing of school ma'ams. My second main subject, English, was really my best subject and should have come as a relief. But once I sat down by the fire in my study, I couldn't get past the first paragraph of a book without falling asleep.

It took me months to finish 'Tom Jones' and 'Tristram Shandy' never got a look in. Eventually though, and in more ways than one, I woke up and became an insatiable reader and collector of recipes and books. It's amazing how motivated a job and salary make you. At twenty-one I was teaching English and Home Economics and enjoying it and becoming an exacting school ma'am myself. But there was something missing.

Lymm Rugby Club provided the relaxed atmosphere where I first met my husband Stuart. Noticing we shared an interest in wildlife, he invited me to join him the next evening to sit up a tree and watch fox cubs. It was our first date. We never looked back. By nature he was a hunter and provider and I wanted to explore the big wide world as well as put my Home Economics into practice.

In our twenties, we skied the alps, sailed the oceans, dived the seas and bought boats where other couples bought furniture. Summer meant freshly-caught lobster, crab and scallops and in winter, pheasants, partridge and rabbits. These favourite recipes are all included here. The term 'organic' was not in use then but we didn't need to be told that what we were eating was the best, most wholesome food.

All this time I was formulating how best to assess, adapt or invent recipes for my ever-growing collection. It was not just a case of cooking the best value dishes for my time, effort, money, health and taste buds but would Stuart like it? In later years, my aching joints led me to recipes using natural, unprocessed ingredients in the dishes I had grown to love and didn't want to give up.

I had to increase my fruit and vegetable intake but I wasn't going to just eat leaves and berries no matter how healthy they were. Everything in moderation or I would decline. Fortunately my interest coincided with media coverage of Paleo type diets for the fashionable and famous and sat well with our love of nature and the countryside.

Here are the results to share with you. As we are urged to eat more vegetables, I have included many recipes to make them (even) more interesting along with salads to suit all occasions. Cutting down on meat is good for us and the planet, so I present a variety of protein substitutes such as halloumi cheese which may be barbecued; very, very tasty feta, red onion and spinach burgers and the Welsh delicacy of vegetarian Glamorgan sausages. Plant-based sauces eliminate the need for processed flour and there are beautiful bread recipes which use the healthiest flours.

Most of my desserts are fruit-based. Nut bases replace pastry bases which, like my favourite the almond base, are simply delicious. I've discovered that rice flour is a great substitute for wheat flour, making the thickening of soups, sauces and stews easier. Spelt flour gives homemade bread a lovely, nutty flavour. It is also easier as it doesn't require kneading.

Fine oatmeal makes a better stuffing than breadcrumbs and also a delicious topping in a crumble pudding. There's a lovely chocolate mousse made with avocados and my latest cake recipes use ground almond or even beetroot instead of flour.

Recipes for pâtés such as liver or smoked fish top the scales for goodness and are satisfying and easy to make. When it's Wimbledon time afternoon tea devotees can bake meringues. Though high in sugar, I just eat a dainty portion topped with cream and fresh strawberries. This moderate approach to diet suits me better than self-denial. Family favourite dishes using meat and fish are included.

My very favourite recipes conjure up happy memories of being in the great outdoors to acquire the food, so much better than queuing in a supermarket. Damson jam evokes the woods and in particular, the home of the spindly, elegant damson tree. Blackberries are the heart of the English hedgerow heralding autumn as do apples which alone or combined make great desserts.

Most magnificent of all, lobster, crabs and scallops conjure memories of underwater swimming with fishes in calm, azure waters abroad or slightly rougher seas at home. Fresh mackerel reminds me of being gently rocked in a boat on the sunlit sea of Aberdaron when landing those silver and navy blue striped delights for tea. Pheasants and partridge have come to us more easily. On winter afternoons, a knock on the back door often signals the welcome sight of a neighbour holding a brace.

I hope these recipes give you as much pleasure as they have given me. I certainly feel healthier for the adjustments I have made to my diet. The joints are less creaky so I can enjoy bat and ball with my grandsons and run for a train if necessary when I go to see them. It is good to feel more in control of what you are eating and widen your mind to foreign cuisine especially the healthy Mediterranean diet.

But there is plenty to enjoy in the traditional British cuisine which I think we underrate. We often neglect the fine ingredients under our nose. So I have included roast dinners and British stews and puddings and a seasonal chart to aid buying cheap fresh food at its seasonal and nutritious best. We are too reliant on getting most foods all year round but an English strawberry in summer smells and tastes so much better than a weary jetlagged strawberry in winter.

Probably my biggest wish or ambitious aim for this cookbook is that it may help to stimulate a deeper appreciation of our wonderful natural world. Re-connecting with nature is now an important issue for mental and physical well-being and for the future of the planet. I hope that the anecdotes herein provide food for thought on this and life in general.

A Celebration of Starters

STARTERS are the burlesque of the culinary world: a lot of tease here and some titillating flesh there. They should prepare you for what is to come and unlike modern starters, not be the main act itself.

Fresh fruit makes a good starter – sweet, juicy, tangy, sumptuous and delectably mouth-watering – whether apricots from Egypt, figs from Lebanon or apples from your own back garden.

I grew up in the 1950s on a post-war diet of porridge, pea soup and hotpot. Fortunately, my father was a greengrocer and every day he placed a basket of fresh fruit on the sideboard just for me: a daily gift which made me very appreciative of fruit and him.

Hill and Glover, a flourishing family business throughout my childhood.
Latchford, Warrington, 1969.

In the Fifties, most people's experience of a starter was soup or port-splashed melon at a family's wedding breakfast. It is easy to laugh now but it prepared you for the roast chicken and sherry trifle to follow. Modern day starters range from Toad in the Hole with gravy to barbecued garlic bread covered in barbecue sauce topped with mozzarella and chilli flakes in a sour cream dip.

What are they preparing you for ? Being sick perhaps or obese. For a healthy, stimulating starter or a treat or a tonic anytime of the day try:

Fresh fruit cocktails or 'mocktails'

Blitz chopped fresh fruit in seconds with a small blender. No need to peel peaches or apples. Add ice and sparkling or still water and serve with a dash of panache: an elegant glass adorned with a simple mint leaf or maraschino cherry skewed on a cocktail stick.

Oriental tiger: a centimetre of ginger, 2 slices pineapple, water to taste (a small stick of celery is optional – *favourite.)*

Hawaiian twist: 1 pineapple slice, 1 tsp lime juice, handful of spinach, 250ml almond juice or water to taste.

Duchess's delight: a slice of melon and pineapple, a handful of spinach, a centimetre of ginger (a stick of celery optional).

Night sight: 1 carrot, a centimetre of ginger, 300ml fresh orange juice.

New Year Promise: 1 carrot, a slice of cooked beetroot, a sweet orange and a handful of kale.

Lemon cooler: quarter a lemon and blitz with some ice cubes. Pour into a jug topped with water and add sugar to taste, up to 100ml. (On a crazily hot day this was once gratefully received by colleagues. All it took was ice cubes, a lemon and a blender.)

To sweeten any of the above either add honey or fruit such as melon, strawberries, apples. To sharpen the taste, add pineapple or tangy orange or lemon juice. Perhaps go lightly on ginger at first.

Smoothies

Not the lechers at the bar but concentrated fruit and vegetable drinks. They owe their thick texture to the addition of either avocado, banana, ice cream or yogurt. However, beware of a sugar overdose as nature's bounty is dangerous in excess. Good combinations which do not have to be accurately measured are:

1 banana, 1 peach, 5 strawberries.

5 strawberries, 1 banana, small carton of yogurt. Add milk to taste if needed.

3 leaves of kale, 1 kiwi, 1 banana, 1 pear, 200ml almond milk, (3-4 ice cubes optional).

1 orange, banana, pear, carrot or slice of pineapple and either 50ml coconut water or plain water.

equal amounts of either strawberry (or use blueberry or cherry instead) with pear, melon and avocado.

sprig of parsley, clump of kale, 1cm ginger, 1 apple or avocado, ½ tsp lemon juice and honey, 3 ice cubes.

If you want a fruity alcoholic cocktail, make a Bellini by half filling the glass with fresh peach or pear juice and a dash of fruit cognac. Top up with prosecco.

Chargrilled melon

Per person, cut two or three slices of fresh honeydew melon and chargrill or brown lightly in a hot frying pan smeared lightly with oil. Arrange slices on a dinner plate in a fan shape and decorate with seasonal fruits and swirls of raspberry coulis (raspberries pureed with a little sugar). Sorbet makes a delightful addition. Decorate with a mint leaf.

Breakfast fresh fruit salads

No two of my fresh fruit salads are the same but all are welcomed by my grandchildren who ask for it at breakfast. I prepare a big bowl the night before using whatever fresh and tinned fruit is available (not frozen fruit as it collapses on thawing.)

The next morning, half asleep, I plonk it on the table and start frying sausages and bacon. More often I serve fresh fruit salad as a dessert but it also makes a good starter. With experience I've learnt to use tinned or bottled fruit syrup for speed. Fresh syrup is best.

Fresh fruit salad with fresh syrup (serves four)

**450g (1lb) seasonal fruit. Aim for a variety of texture, flavour and colour such as orange, blackberry, apple and peach.
250g (½ pint) syrup made from water and 100g (4oz) sugar**

Dissolve sugar in pan with water and bring to boil before cooling and adding any peeling, seeds and bits of core to infuse the flavours (along with bay leaf or clove if desired.) Infuse for at least 10 minutes in warmth before sieving. Place washed and prepared fruit in serving dish.

To prevent browning, peeled fruit may be rubbed with lemon and/or placed under non peeled fruit. If using liqueur add now but remember not to give it the kids for breakfast! 1-2 tablespoons of Grand Marnier is good. Stop to enjoy the fragrance. Strain cooled syrup through sieve and over fruit. Keep chilled.

Pâtés

When served in individual pots with dry toast cut into triangles or with pitta bread, home-made pâtés make tasty starters or salad accompaniments. They are so easy and satisfying to make, you wonder why we would buy shop ones. Often all they involve is mashing a key ingredient with the possible addition of either (or all of) lemon juice, seasoning, cream cheese and flavourings.

So simple avocado pâté

Mix ripe avocado flesh with cream cheese or mascarpone in roughly equal amounts. Reminder to self: mascarpone is a pure cheese (no additives) so it doesn't keep fresh forever.

Even more simple avocado pâté

Mash avocado flesh (optional: add lemon juice – good for preserving and mild chilli powder) and serve with toast.

If the avocado is perfectly ripe, and buying and storing avocados soon teaches this, simply slice the flesh onto the bread or toast, with or without chilli powder or lemon for a great breakfast.

It may also be topped with a little fried bacon and mushroom. I often pinch a slither of my husband's irresistible smelling bacon to make my happiness complete.

"Ripeness is all."

William Shakespeare's King Lear

(I know. He wasn't talking about avocados.)

Kipper pâté

Mix equal amounts of filleted kippers with sufficient cream cheese or mascarpone to get a paste consistency. A drop of lemon juice may be added. Divine!

Look out for proper smoked kippers rather than the inferior dyed ones. Fresh or smoked mackerel works well too.

Smoked mackerel and smoked salmon pâté

Good on toast or sandwiches and freezes well. Mix flaked smoked mackerel with equal amounts of finely chopped smoked (or cooked) salmon and cream cheese. When well blended add a teaspoon of lemon juice.

Smoked mackerel and horseradish pâté

Blitz all together with a little black pepper:

> **1 smoked fillet**
> **40g cream cheese**
> **35g crème fraiche**
> **1-2 tsp horseradish**
> **squeeze of lemon juice**

Quick tasty liver pâté

(This freezes well. In fact, they all do.)

Shallow fry slices of liver, preferably lamb's, till cooked. Cut up small and place in liquidiser with enough dashes of double cream, very strong flavourings such as Worcester sauce, mustard, Greek kumquat liqueur and seasoning to get a great taste and spreadable texture. Garnish with gherkins. When making liver and onions for tea, cook excess in preparation for whizzing up a pâté next day.

Over to Greece
(because of their gorgeous starters)

I was quite young when I fell in love with Greece, about twenty-one. I had been watching a film about a runaway couple's island-hopping adventure.

Could the sky and sea really be that blue, the trees so green and the islands so close? When I was forty I discovered it was true.

We visited Corfu with Club 18-30, the only last-minute holiday available. To get away from the ghetto blasters, a motorbike was needed. We loved it so much that for the next thirty years we zoomed round the islands, soaking up the sunshine, the thyme-scented breeze and simple, gorgeous, fresh food amidst the easy going, good-natured hospitality of the Greeks.

The mezzes listed here are best served with hot sunshine. If that is in short supply, turn up the heating. Play some Greek music. Relax.

Hummus

	100g - 150g tinned chickpeas
optional extra:	**cooked sweet potato**
	25g tahini or three tbsp sesame seeds
	1 clove garlic
	juice of a lemon
	1½ tbsp olive oil

Blitz chickpeas with tahini (sesame paste), lemon juice, salt and pepper. Serve with slices of warm pitta bread and olives.

Cheaper than a donkey, a good way to explore Cephalonia if you're an experienced motorcyclist. Sami, 1997.

Quick Pitta Bread (serves two)

On Greek street corners you are never far from a gyros bar and for under 3 Euros, a gyros makes a perfect lunch. It consists of a light pitta wrapped in a cone shape, stuffed with lettuce, tomato, thinly sliced red onion, a sprinkling of freshly chopped oregano, tzatziki and freshly fried hot chicken or pork.

(A quick tzatziki can be made by adding garlic salt and chopped oregano to Greek yogurt. I expect there is a law against this in Greece as catering recipes have to be exact and must use fresh food.)

100g (4oz) Greek-style full fat yogurt
100g SR flour*
pinch of salt

***or plain flour + 1tsp baking power**

In a bowl mix yogurt with SR flour. Pat into a round shape and on a board roll lightly till about ½ cm thick and 27cm (10 ½-inch) diameter. Cut the circle in half for ease of handling but add both sides to a little olive oil heated in a big frying pan. Brown both sides. Keep warm.

To serve, shape into a cone with a slight overlap. Stuff the wide top with gyros contents as above or the filling of your choice.

Flat bread (makes 3)

125g white bread flour or spelt
¼ tsp salt
pinch ground black pepper
30ml olive oil
55ml warm water

Weigh flour. Add salt and pepper. Mix olive oil with warm water and slowly stir into seasoned flour to make a soft pliable dough. (Add a little more water or flour if necessary.) Use a lightly floured rolling pin, shape into rounds less than ½ cm thick. Fry in an olive oiled frying pan for 3-4 minutes or more each side. Layer bread between kitchen paper. Serve warm.

Taramasalata (Fish roe paste)

This is tastier than hummus. Once I bought tinned 'pressed cod roe' by mistake but carried on regardless. It tasted great especially when left in the fridge overnight but fresh or pure roe is better.

I wouldn't be fussy about the type of roe. See what the fishmonger suggests. All homemade is better than bought paste which may have as little as 6% roe.

150g preserved fish roe (ask a fishmonger)
2-3 tbsp lemon juice
250g white stale bread (or use mash potato)
½ finely chopped onion (optional but good)
small wine glass olive oil

optional: **crushed walnuts or olives to garnish**

Soak bread in water till soft. Drain well by squeezing with your hands. Using a blender, blitz it all together to get a smooth, creamy paste. It is too tasty, too easy and too healthy to save for holidays and it keeps well in the freezer if you have to wait for the British sun to appear.

Traditional Greek music goes straight to my heart and makes me want to dance. Fortunately, there's little corruption of their culture to suit tourists. You can admire the Aegean without being blasted by heavy metal.

Tzatziki

1 small cucumber
2 garlic cloves, pressed
1 tsp each olive oil and vinegar
500g full fat Greek yogurt
salt and ground black pepper

Grate cucumber. Take a handful at a time and squeeze out its unwanted juice with your hands. (This simple but effective technique
was shown to me by a Greek chef.) Stir the grated cucumber into
the yogurt along with other ingredients. Sprinkle with fresh oregano or dill, finely chopped. Plop an olive in the centre if you
must. Enjoy with pitta or crusty bread.

Garlic yogurt? Peter Kaye might say. But to me it evokes lush
green islands of pine trees, lemon groves, turquoise crystal seas
with gently lapping waves and the music of the balalaika and mandolin: heaven. However, I must concede that it is a hot weather
dish and like Ouzo it fails to seduce if the temperature drops below
twenty degrees.

A Speciality of Soups

FROM Tennessee to New Orleans, lunch menus offer you a fresh soup and salad combo. What a good idea. These two simple dishes are the easiest way to eat a concentration of vegetables, something we are constantly urged to do.

More importantly, soup has always fortified, caressed and sustained mankind. Be it a delicate, daintily served crab soup in a Chinese restaurant or a hearty robust Scotch broth, soup can awaken the dullest appetite or satisfy the deepest hunger.

Once, in the middle of winter, we braved ice, fog and snow to get to a big party, arriving like frosted Christmas trees, a whiter shade of pale. We sat down to eat and in unison with others, rolled back our soup spoons in anticipation of a welcome hot broth. But there was a collective silent shock and a general recoiling.

Ugh! It wasn't too salty, too hot or too sweet. It was too cold: ice cold. When the initial disappointment subsided, it tasted pleasant but the horror lingered. Cold soup is lovely in the Spanish heat but in Britain it might be best to announce that the soup is cold, possibly with a visible ice cube or two.

> ### "Life's fundamental principle is the satisfaction of the stomach."
>
> *Epicurus*

(Perhaps Epicurus should have got out more.)

Quick light soups

Gazpacho (serves two-three)

The quickest ever. Simply chop and blitz together saving some chunks for decoration.

½ green pepper
½ red onion
some small ice cubes
1 clove garlic
3-4 tomatoes
salt, pepper
¼ cucumber
1-2 tbsp of red wine vinegar
1-2 tbsp of olive oil
optional: passata (sieved tomato)

I prefer the soup a little chunky and with a distinctive red and green contrast. Some passata may be added to achieve a dominant red colour. Serve very chilled in a hot climate garnished with bay leaves or mint and ice cube or two.

Beetroot and sweet potato (serves two-three)

This soup has a great flavour and clean taste. It freezes well and is ever so good for you.

½ onion, finely chopped
1½ sweet potatoes, cubed
(or 1 medium white and 1 small sweet potato)
1½ cooked beetroots, cubed
1 tbsp olive oil
250ml beef, chicken or vegetable stock
300ml water, more if needed
2 tsp ground cumin, a bay leaf and seasoning
garnish: some Greek yogurt and a handful of walnut pieces

Sauté onion in oil and when soft add sweet potato and beetroot and sauté again for 3 minutes. Add stock, a bay leaf, a little salt and black pepper and enough water to cover vegetables.

Simmer for 30 minutes. Remove bay leaf and blitz with hand blender. Thin the consistency with water. Serve with a small dollop of yogurt and a sprinkling of walnuts.

Watercress and spinach soup (serves three-four)

This recipe allows you to use up watercress and spinach from those massive supermarket bags when you tire of eating them as a salad. Light soups such as this are an exception to the rule that a good stock is needed.

> **15g butter**
> **salt and black pepper**
> **2-3 spring onions, finely chopped**
> **250ml boiling water**
> **300g watercress, washed**
> **250ml ice cubes**
> **100g spinach, washed**
> **cream, crème fraiche**
> **or: Greek yogurt to swirl**

Sweat onion in melted butter 3 minutes. Turn up heat and add cress and spinach and wilt for 2 minutes. Add boiling water, seasoning and boil 2 minutes. Remove.

Add ice to stop the cooking process and retain colour, taste and texture. Blitz all, preferably with a hand held blender. Re-heat before serving. Optional: serve with a twirl of cream.

Valpellinese cabbage soup (serves four)

This simple but hearty delicious traditional soup of the Italian alps might be made with cooked potatoes if the thought of soggy bread is unpalatable to you. Personally, I like it.

> **1 big savoy cabbage (about 650g)**
> **200g stale bread or crusty bread**
> **275g Cheddar or fontina cheese**
> **50g butter**
> **300ml chicken stock**
> **300ml cabbage liquor**

Slice and chop cabbage into mouthful size pieces. Wash and boil
3-4 minutes. Cube bread. Drain cabbage and keep liquor. In a
flameproof casserole or big pan place a layer of cooked cabbage, a
layer of bread and a layer of cheese. Repeat. Press down and pour
over stock and the melted butter. Stir, taste, season and serve hot.

Soups requiring stock

Stock makes a soup substantial, especially if you buy the best possible stock cubes or better still, make your own stock. It is not difficult. Trust me. It is only a matter of boiling bones in water. For
example, after you have eaten a roast chicken, take a big pan (preferably a pressure cooker to reduce cooking time to a third) add
bones, skin and leftovers.

Cover with water and boil for at least an hour (or pressure cook for
20 minutes), topping up the water if necessary. Cool and then
sieve the extract into a jug. (To freeze, pour stock into an ice cube
tray. Or pour stock into a freezer bag or box to make a thin layer
which will defrost easily.)

Summer Pea (serves two)

	200g fresh (or frozen) peas
	1 big spring onion, chopped
	12g butter
	400ml stock and a little milk
optional:	1 tsp freshly chopped mint
	garnish with a tsp of double cream

Fry chopped onion lightly in butter till golden and soft and then
add other ingredients and
boil for 5 minutes before
liquidising with a hand
blender.

(A little shredded lettuce
may be added with the
peas.)

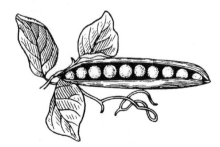

Mushroom *(serves two-three)*

1 small onion, chopped finely
200g clean, sliced mushrooms
25g butter
500ml chicken stock (a little milk optional)
25g cornflour
seasoning*

* variations include using spring onions, adding chestnuts, sherry or thyme or all three.

Gently fry onions till soft then add mushrooms and a sprinkling of salt and continue cooking for 5 minutes till soft and wilted. Add stock and simmer for 15 minutes. Thicken with a little cornflour blended with water, stirring well as you bring it to boil. Serve with a dollop of fresh cream or crème fraiche.

Green vegetable *(serves two-three)*

200g mix of broccoli, green beans, broad beans, peas
1 crushed garlic clove
half an onion, finely chopped
25g butter or 1 tbsp olive oil
400ml stock with some milk added
chopped fresh parsley, oregano, rosemary or thyme
1 good tsp cumin

Melt butter and fry onion till soft then add the rest of the vegetables, garlic and sauté a few minutes. Add stock and salt and pepper and simmer for 10 minutes or so before coarsely blending.

> "The pleasure of rediscovering
> each season's vegetables."
>
> *Elizabeth David*

(An Englishwoman, educated at the Sorbonne, Elizabeth David taught the British how to enjoy eating olive oil, even on lettuce. Before the 1960s, olive oil was only used here for removing wax from ears and most Brits would have nothing to do with eating it!)

Substantial Main Course Soups

If you are new to Britain, some days are cold, dark and depressing. A hot substantial soup makes the perfect antidote as does an open fire and a good book.

Leek and potato (serves four)

25g butter and a little olive oil
2 large leeks (400g), finely sliced and rinsed through a sieve
1 large potato (200g) peeled and chopped small
600ml chicken stock and 150ml milk

(Variation: for a chowder liquidise with 50g sweetcorn then add chunks of ham.)

Sauté vegetables in melted butter for about 5 minutes. (Stop to smell the delicious aroma). Add stock and simmer about 15 minutes till vegetables are soft and cooked. Serve with a little dollop of fresh cream if desired.

"Eat well, stay fit, die anyway."

Sri Lankan kurakkan kanha breakfast soup

Also known as Sri Lankan porridge, this soup was in the breakfast buffet in our Sri Lankan hotel and they were kind enough to give me the recipe. It tastes nourishing yet is simple to make.

I have not accessed kurakkan flour in the UK yet, only 'ragi' which is made from highly nutritious millet (fancy budgies being better fed than most of us.) It is light brown in colour whereas the hotel soup was white – so not quite right.

2 tbsp kurakkan flour
2 tbsp coconut milk powder
1 cup of water
1½ cups of water

Add the cup of water to flour and mix well. Stir over a low heat. As it thickens add the coconut milk powder which has been mixed in 1½ cups of water. Add a little salt if desired. Bring slowly to the boil, after which it is ready to eat.

Mother's Ham and Pea Soup (serves four)

My mother was a busy lady who worked in the saloon, a small coal house next to our tiny kitchen. On pain of death, we were not allowed to open the adjoining door, though I used to listen at the keyhole.

She always seemed to be talking about me. 'Jennifer is learning the violin now. Jennifer is having Latin lessons etc.' This image was at odds with the scruffy savage in the garden playing cowboys and Indians with brother George.

Through him I developed survival skills, learning not to panic when pushed in the pond or how to untie myself from a tree before his fire got hold, or keeping perfectly still against the garage wooden wall whilst he threw knives round me like we saw at the circus.

How I came out unscathed is a miracle. But we knew never to disturb mother when she was with a client in the saloon. Mother's

Mother and daughter dressed up for the beach. New Brighton, 1959.

cooking was limited to hotpot and pea soup. Sometimes a ham was added so the delicious stock formed the basis of the soup. Later I could sneak into the larder and rip off juicy chunks of ham to gobble.

More often the pea soup was cooked with bacon ribs which George and I slowly gnawed from one end of the bone to the other. They knew how to keep children quiet in those days. Another trick was being made to stay at the table until you had finished your meal and then you had to clean your plate with bread and butter.

I see the sense of it now: it ensured you were full and it made the washing up easier.

220g dried split green peas
1 onion, finely chopped
small ham hock or shank
- cover in water, soak overnight
900ml (1½ pints) water
1-2 carrots, chopped fine
extra water if topping up is needed

Optional: 1 stick of celery, finely sliced and mint and thyme

Soak peas according to packet directions. I usually do it overnight. Come on. It's not that hard. (Talking to myself!) In the morning, whilst feeling smug that you / I actually did it, drain and rinse the peas then place into a large pan. Add drained and rinsed ham hock, onion and carrot.

Pour water over and bring to the boil. Skim off scum. Cover and simmer 45 minutes to 1 hour or pressure cook 15-20 minutes till meat is tender. Season. Shred or chop ham and add to soup before serving this wholesome and delicious dish hot. Note: a 2lb ham needs 20 minutes per lb plus 20 minutes ie 1 hour boiling. Or 20 minutes pressure cooking.)

Bacon and lentil (serves four)

> **25g butter and oil**
> **350g fresh tomatoes**
> **(or 400g can of tomatoes)**
> **1 medium onion, chopped**
> **600ml chicken or bacon stock**
> **100g bacon, chopped small**
> **salt and pepper**
> **chopped herbs (parsley, thyme,**
> **oregano)**
> **240g can of cooked lentils**
> **(or 100g dried lentils, soaked)**

Fry onion till soft. Add bacon and fry together 2 minutes. Add stock, tomatoes, salt and pepper, herbs and lentils. Bring to the boil and simmer 20 minutes for tinned and at least 40 minutes extra if using dry lentils. Liquidise, preferably with a hand held blender.

Cullen Skink – utterly simple, utterly delicious. (serves four+)

Not Scottish for bashing a skunk on the head but a soup now usually made with finnan haddie (smoked haddock.) I believe Cullen is a fishing port in Scotland and Skink an old Scots word for shin which was boiled to make stock.

And ancient 'Braveheart' wives up and down the Scottish coast, when not spinning wool, or burning porridge, repairing their man's kilt, practising their fiddle or lamenting that their secret lover had made them pregnant and turned into a seal, (loneliness does funny things to the mind), then they were making this soup with whatever fish came their way.

> **400g skinned, smoked haddock**
> **50g butter**
> **bay leaf**
> **1 medium onion, chopped fine**
> **handful of flat, chopped parsley**
> **250g potato, finely cubed**
> **black pepper**
> **445ml water**
> **255ml milk**

In a saucepan, gently sauté onion in butter a few minutes till soft and golden. Add potatoes and sauté 2 minutes. Add water and simmer 10 minutes till all is soft. In the meantime poach fish in milk with bay leaf for 3 minutes. Add fish milk liquor to saucepan and parsley leaves.

Remove bay leaf. When ready to serve, flake fish and heat through with all together for no more than 5 minutes being careful not to overcook fish. Season with black pepper and also salt if necessary. (A dollop of double cream to serve is optional but very nice.)

Bouillabaisse (serves six)

This is a French version of Cullen Skink. The French and the Scottish have a lot in common, mainly a history of fighting the English. It is odd that the English lack national fish dishes: nothing to mark us out as a seafaring nation island other than the fish and chippy and the man who occasionally enters a pub with a basket of cockles.

Even the Victorians looked down on oysters as a poor man's food. When will we ever learn? Bouillabaisse is a beautiful soup. It also makes a delicious stew by adding cooked potato chunks.

2-3lb (1kg) mix of white fish like cod or haddock, oily fish, eg salmon, tuna or shellfish such as mussels, prawns
3 tbsp olive oil
1-2 onions, sliced
1-2 leeks, washed well & sliced thinly
2 cloves garlic, minced
3 large tomatoes, chopped
1 bay leaf
3 sprigs thyme
a little fennel or ouzo
½ tsp turmeric (or saffron threads)
1 tsp salt
¼ tsp black pepper
long strip of orange zest
1 litre fish stock / water

Heat olive oil and gently sauté garlic and onions, leeks and fennel for about 10 minutes till softened. Add tomatoes, bay leaf, thyme, turmeric and orange zest.

Add stock and cubed fish and any fish shells. Simmer gently until fish is cooked (turns opaque) a maximum of 10 minutes. Serve with crusty bread.

Cullen Skink has many fans in the culinary world with some even suggesting it's the world's best soup. I would give it second place. It hurts me to say this but Bouillabaisse is my winner.

I think it may have something to do with the image of fishermen sitting on their boats in the Med and, having mended their nets, a fire on the beach is lit, a pot heated and whatever is catch of the day thrown in along with shells and a glass of Pernod (or Ouzo if we are in Greece and then Antony Quinn dances on the quayside.)

All is fresh and different, so precisely unpredictable in flavour but predictably gorgeous. And eaten in the last remaining, warming rays of a golden sunset. That's living. I can get all of that from a bowl of soup!

Chowders

American chowders have all the goodness in one pot which saves time, fuss and washing up. Serve alone or with bread and cheese for a substantial main meal.

Fish chowder (serves four heartily)

25g chopped bacon or pancetta
500ml milk
15g butter
25g polenta (optional)
2 sticks celery, thinly sliced
1 tbsp oil
500ml fish stock
250g waxy potatoes, finely chopped
390g chunks fresh fish (fish pie mix)
1 tbsp chopped fresh chives

In a large pan melt butter and oil, fry pancetta 4 minutes till gold and crispy. Add polenta and cook 1 minute. Add celery and potato and cook for 5 minutes till soft.

Pour on milk and fish stock. Boil then simmer for 15 minutes or more till potato is soft and cooked. Add fish. Cook 5 minutes more till fish is opaque. Garnish with chives and serve with crusty bread.

Quick sweetcorn and mackerel chowder

(serves three heartily or water down a bit for four)

50g cashew nuts
200g sweetcorn, fresh or tinned
1 tbsp chopped leaves of parsley
and chives
200g mackerel, fresh or smoked
black pepper
1 pint chicken stock

I love this recipe. The soup tastes great. It's lightning quick to make and very healthy.

Boil fresh or frozen sweetcorn in the pint of stock for 5 minutes. (Not necessary for tinned.) Mix your cooked or tinned corn with cashew nuts and herbs (save some for garnish) and blitz. When using a hand-held blender in the pan, watch the flex doesn't go near the hot hob.

Add flaked mackerel (or flaked chicken or crab if preferred.) Stir well. If using raw fish or meat, heat for 5 minutes in soup till cooked, otherwise just add cooked flesh and bring soup to boiling point. Keep hot. Garnish with chopped herbs and serve with crusty bread and black pepper.

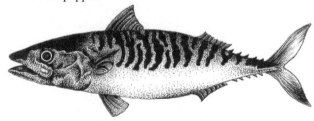

Smoked haddock, sweet potato and prawn chowder

(serves about three)	**175g smoked, skinned haddock**
	150ml milk
	1 leek (or celery) sliced and washed
	1 small onion, diced
	30g butter
	1 tbsp or more olive oil
	150g potatoes, diced
	100g sweet potato, diced
	300ml fish stock
	1 bay leaf
	50g washed, cold water prawns
	a little crème fraiche (or cream)
	some chives

Simmer haddock 3 minutes each side in milk. Rest. Fry onion and
leeks in oil and butter for 10 minutes till soft. Add potatoes to
glaze them. Stir in stock and bay leaf. Simmer 20-30 minutes till
very tender. Evenly flake fish and about 3 minutes before serving
add to soup along with prawns. Heat through. Serve in bowls garnished with bacon or ham pieces, a dollop of crème fraiche or
cream and a sprinkling of chopped chives.

Making up your own soup recipe

Soup is a great way of using up leftovers. If you are cooking from
scratch, two or three fresh harmonious ingredients are all that is
needed. Imagine finding carrot in your leek and potato soup. Not
needed. Many delicious soups can be made in minutes. Before you
take your coat off after that bracing walk in the countryside melt a
little butter and oil, add some frozen chopped onions on a low heat
and start gently sweating, that's the onions, of course.

When soft add other finely-chopped vegetables and 'fat steam' a
few minutes till soft. Add stock and seasoning and simmer till
cooked. If you like a smooth soup, a hand blender can be held over
the pan. Don't let the flex near the heat or Blackpool Illuminations
will arrive early.

A Succession of Salads

The back of the shop was a flurry of activity with a lorry for market trips and a van for home deliveries. Latchford, 1954.

Insider knowledge

IN the greengrocer's shop my father managed, a wooden crate of unshelled peas had just arrived yet they were wilting and attracting millions of little flies. 'Do you know vegetables sweat?' my father asked.

I placed my hand in the middle of the peas and was amazed at the heat generated. 'Once picked and piled together vegetables collapse, especially in a damp atmosphere,' he said and explained that these peas must be dried quickly.

Good management of salad vegetables means reducing damp, air and light. Ideally, salad is home grown and picked, washed and served immediately at its crispiest and freshest. If you buy bags of salad, open and place folded kitchen paper inside to absorb moisture, seal and place in the fridge. You'll be amazed how quickly the paper gets damp and needs changing but delighted how much longer the salad keeps.

In Costa Rica I saw whole melons and pineapples stored in the big hotel fridge. I now do likewise. Plenty of fridge space helps the chef.

Refrigeration means we now enjoy better salads from crunchy salsas to hot main meal salads with enough beef, chicken or ham tossed in to satisfy a hardened carnivore.

That's got to be better than the Fifties' offering of a bitter-tasting lettuce leaf, a tomato and a bottle of help-yourself salad cream. But in those days only 15% of households had a fridge.

Hot Main Meal Salads

With the best will in the world, eating a salad on a cold winter's day when wind rattles your frosty windows is daunting. But serve the key ingredients hot and salad is a different story.

Basically, prepare the leafy green bits of whatever you like such as lettuce and celery and cook the protein part like eggs, bacon, fish or chicken and add it hot to the salad before tossing in a dressing. (See page 31).

Chicken Caesar salad's main ingredients are cooked chicken, leaves of romaine, cos or web lettuce and anchovies.

Add croutons made by freshly frying white cubes of bread in olive oil till golden and then dry with kitchen paper. Toss in some Parmesan (or Cheddar) shavings.

The dressing is a mayonnaise base with the addition of small amounts of mustard, Worcester sauce and black pepper. I like to tone the dressing down by mixing in some olive oil and plain Greek yogurt (or water) but some prefer it richer with the addition of cream cheese or anchovy oil.

Other possible additions are garlic, white wine vinegar or lemon juice.

Mackerel, cucumber, celery and gooseberry salsa

> **Per person: a mackerel fillet**
> **dash of balsamic vinegar**
> **50g prepared gooseberries**
> **celery stick**
> **chunk of cucumber, chopped finely**

Prepare gooseberries (wash, top and tail) and simmer for a few minutes with a minimum of water and enough sugar to coat fruit. Season and add a dash of balsamic vinegar. Combine finely chopped celery and cucumber. Add to cooled gooseberry sauce. Fry or grill mackerel a few minutes on both sides till the edges are brown and crispy. Serve with salsa.

Smoked mackerel may be heated up (or served cold) then flaked and tossed with a mix of chopped celery, apple, crisp shredded cos or gem lettuce and some mild horseradish sauce. This is an excellent salad. Carnivores like this too. (A variation is smoked mackerel with celery, apple, horseradish and a dressing of soya sauce, honey and sesame seeds.)

Bacon and avocado salad is made by stirring fried bacon pieces that are still warm into a prepared shredded gem lettuce salad of quartered cherry tomatoes and avocado. Serve with a mustard dressing (see page 31). A similar recipe is to mix avocado with cooked, chopped bacon and blueberries. Place on a rocket base and pour over a dressing of blueberries mixed with oil, vinegar, mustard and honey. Yum, yum.

Prawn and pineapple salad (serves four)

> **half an iceberg lettuce, shredded**
> **3 fresh pineapple slices, chopped**
> **(mangoes will do)**
> **2 sticks celery, chopped**
> **400g prawns**
> **2 tbsp sunflower oil or sesame seed oil**
> **12 small, boiled new potatoes (450g)**
> **1 dssp soy sauce**
> **1 tsp honey**

Fill a salad bowl with shredded lettuce and chopped celery. Heat sunflower oil and stir in fresh pineapple chunks and cook lightly. Next add boiled, small or chopped, new potatoes and heat through gently for a few minutes. Then add the prawns and stir fry 3 minutes till pink if they are fresh and therefore grey ones. Remove pan from heat as soon as they turn pink. Ready cooked pink prawns just need to be gently heated through at the end to avoid overcooking. Add a dash of honey and soya sauce. Add pan contents to salad and stir it all thoroughly and serve immediately.

I made this dish up on a balmy summer's evening when we ate in the garden with friends who were joining us for a Blues evening in a local village. Mojo Buford, Muddy Waters' harmonica player, was the star turn. He had turned eighty and despite the heat, wore a black woollen hat and overcoat and a big warm smile. His harmonica playing was sublime and we danced to the livelier numbers. What a perfect evening.

"If music be the food of love, play on."

Shakespeare's Twelfth Night

Cold Main Meal Salad Combinations

Salads, just like you and me, need dressing. If in doubt about your choice, make a simple dressing of equal amounts of olive oil and balsamic vinegar in a jug or bottle and shake to form an emulsion. Or use equal amounts of olive oil and lemon juice and a little seasoning. Just before eating, shake the dressing and apply lightly to salad. Here are some tasty combinations:

Black and blue salad: Mix shredded lettuce, slices of celery and broken walnuts with black or red grapes and blue cheese. How I love this combination! Splendid. (Vary with figs instead of grapes.)

Feta, peach and avocado with spring onions, spinach leaves, some coriander and French dressing.

Greek salad consists of a thin base of shredded lettuce supporting a layer of sliced tomatoes, cucumbers and red onions topped with a slice of feta cheese sprinkled with oregano. Toss in some black olives for taste and to increase the stunning primary colour contrast of pure white feta against crimson tomatoes and luscious lettuce. A feta compli!

Kale, pecans, avocado, apples are delicious when lightly mixed with Greek yogurt thinned with a little olive oil.

Feta, avocado and smoked mackerel mix well with horseradish, celery and apple.

Flaked smoked mackerel mixes with handfuls of washed watercress, sliced spring onion and thinly sliced radishes (optional toasted sesame seeds). Dress with equal amounts of soy sauce, sesame oil and lemon juice with a dash of ginger (paste or a sprinkle of finely-chopped fresh ginger) and a light touch of sugar or honey.

Caesar salad consists of Cos, gem or romaine lettuce leaves, anchovies, croutons and cheese shavings of Parmesan or Cheddar with a strong mustard mayonnaise to which hot or cold cooked chicken chunks are often added.

Cooked chicken and melon chunks work well with elderflower and tarragon dressing.

Cooked chicken and mango chunks on a bed of lettuce with a French dressing is divine if the chicken is organic free range and the mango just ripe.

Cooked chicken breasts (two) cubed and added to chunks of melon and avocado and sprigs of watercress and/or shredded lettuce leaves is good. Coat with the following blended ingredients: white wine vinegar, 1 tsp elderflower cordial, 40ml oil, 35g single cream, 1 dessertspoon finely-chopped tarragon and salt and pepper.

Coronation chicken salad is freshly cooked boneless chicken cut into chunks and mixed with apricots and/or almonds and mayonnaise and plain yogurt. Stir in some curry powder. One time I used fresh double cream instead of yogurt. It was lovely. I have also discovered it is lovely with just yogurt and mayo possibly thinned slightly with olive oil and then seasoned.

Salad Niçoise consists of cooked French runner beans, tuna chunks, halved cherry tomatoes, black olives, new potatoes, quartered boiled eggs. It is served on a bed of gem lettuce with an anchovy dressing made by blending tomato juice, red wine vinegar, capers, garlic, anchovy fillets (and anchovy oil if wished) basil, olive oil and seasoning. The vegetables may be warmed if the weather is cold.

Salad as an accompaniment

Rather than cooking vegetables it is sometimes quicker and tastier to serve a salad as the accompaniment.

Green: self-explanatory – any combination of lettuce, cucumber, salad leaves and celery.

Summer salad: add sliced radishes and possibly halved strawberries to the green salad above.

Fruity salad: lettuce, currants or raisins, walnut pieces and avocado dressed with honey, balsamic vinegar, lemon juice and olive oil.

Waldorf salad was first conjured, I believe, by a chef at The Waldorf Hotel, New York, with the only ingredients he had left at midnight when a salad was ordered. On a bed of shredded lettuce place apple chunks, sliced celery and walnuts, and cubes of cheese lightly coated with a mayonnaise and yogurt dressing. Sultanas or raisins are an optional extra.

Coleslaw: shredded carrot and white cabbage with a dressing. (Additions may include apple, sultanas, nuts, spring onion.) Celeriac may also be shredded finely and used instead or alongside cabbage.

Deep South slaw: mix ¼ finely chopped big white cabbage with 3-4 tbsp mayonnaise. Add a teaspoon each of olive oil, cider vinegar and mustard. (Grated hard cheese is optional.) Season. This is my favourite coleslaw.

English winter slaw is a good mix of apple slices, red cabbage and celery with grated celeriac, carrot and raw beetroot, sultanas, French dressing and seasoning. It is often served at Christmas time.

Incidentally, 'coleslaw', according to my research, derives from the Dutch words: kool meaning cabbage and sla meaning salad. I'm so glad that's sorted.

Guacamole

Accompanies Mexican dishes like chilli con carne which may also include sour cream and tortilla chips.

1 large ripe avocado
juice of a lime or lemon
2 spring onions, finely chopped
1 large tomato quartered, deseeded and chopped finely.
optional: 2 tbsp chopped coriander
optional: 1 tsp sweet chilli sauce

Cut avocado in half and scrape the flesh from the avocado. (You get adept at this after a while.) Add the juice and mash with a fork. Add spring onions and optional red pepper chopped along with tomato and coriander.

Salsa

The basic salsa is composed of mixed, finely chopped tomatoes, onions and peppers, a little salt and a little lime (or lemon) juice or red wine vinegar – traditional Mexican ingredients. Salsa's sharp, fresh taste complements many dishes.

Variations include the addition of garlic, avocado, mango, black beans and sweetcorn. My favourite mix is tomatoes, mango, spring onions and black beans. Limes have a wonderful flavour that is well worth getting to know.

Salad dressings

TRAVELLING abroad in the Sixties and Seventies, salad dressing was a revelation. At home, we had HP sauce or ketchup on the table. Abroad, they had a bottle of oil and a bottle of vinegar: do-it-yourself French dressing.

How right they were as a simple French dressing of oil and vinegar enhances the taste and texture of a salad and also provides the best nutrients to aid vitamin C absorption. However, we Brits looked rather shocked at these often greasy sets of bottles. Wasn't salad cream on salad enough?

Today we have graduated to mayonnaise which we put on everything, even chips and the fact that the continental bottle duo still doesn't appear on English restaurant tables suggests progress is slow. At home, we should be quicker to knock up a French dressing in a little glass screw-top bottle, ready to shake whenever we serve a salad. Now where did I put that perfect little bottle for my French dressing?

Go easy. A very light dressing only is needed, or the salad can often be drowned. I prefer the healthy restraint shown abroad. In the French quarter of New Orleans, the cabbage in the coleslaw remains dominant, making it crunchier and healthier. To keep control of the dressing on a salad when eating out here, one may always ask for it to be served separately in a jug, please.

French dressing: two parts olive oil to one part vinegar with salt and pepper. Place in a screw top jar and shake before applying as the emulsion formed is temporary. (Optional extras are crushed garlic and brown sugar and wine or lemon juice can substitute the vinegar.)

Slimmer's dressing: whisk a little olive oil into some plain yogurt and/or a little water. Water dominates many bought low-calorie dressings so you can water down your own dressing if required without having to pay for it.

Lemon and honey dressing: juice of a lemon, 2 tbsp clear honey, pepper to taste.

Mustard dressing: 1 tbsp each of oil and vinegar and 1 tsp each of mustard paste and clear honey.

Caesar style: basically throw together anything and everything used for flavouring such as salt, pepper, garlic, lemon juice, mustard, Worcester sauce, Dijon mustard and either French dressing, mayonnaise or a dollop of healthy Greek yogurt or a dollop of cream cheese.

Slaw dressing: mayonnaise, cider vinegar, mustard, grated cheese, a little olive oil and seasoning.

Blue cheese dressing: 1 tbsp mayonnaise, 2 tbsp soured cream, 12g (½ oz) blue cheese.

Combine the above and eat with restraint as those delicious saturated fats may be heart attack inducing!

Wild garlic mayonnaise: finely chop or snip washed leaf and stir into mayonnaise. Goes so well with boiled eggs for salads or sandwiches or when added to butter for steaks or to French dressing. Go easy, it's subtle but strong. Also known as ramsoms, collect the leaves before the white flowers frock the woods.

Anchovy dressing: blend tomato juice, red wine vinegar, capers, garlic, anchovy fillets, basil, olive oil and seasoning.

Like women, the best salads are well dressed and French in style.

A Virtue of Vegetables

THE BRITISH culinary sin used to be boiling vegetables to death. Now we understand 'al dente' instead of 'al morte' so we don't boil for quite so long. If you do boil vegetables try to reduce the liquor rather than throw it down the drain or use it in a gravy or sauce. This conserves the water soluble vitamin C.

Enlightened chefs may choose to fry, steam, grill or microwave. The microwave is useful for small portions of little vegetables like frozen peas or green beans as they cook in about 2 minutes.

Microwave cooking

This retains vitamins which is after all an important reason why we eat vegetables. Place prepared vegetables in a microwave dish and splash with water. Cover with a lid or punctured cling wrap to cook in a third of boiling time with no pan to wash.

When re-heating food in the microwave, test if it is hot enough by taking it out and placing the palm just above the food. It should feel hot to your hovering hand.

NB Avoid over-heating foods like tomato soup which retain heat (having a higher specific heat) and may burn the mouth.

Cooked vegetables as an accompaniment

Microwaving kale, cabbage, peas, broccoli and cauliflower florets, according to many instructions, may take as little as 1½ minutes but I prefer my cabbage fairly well cooked so I chop it fine and cook for 2-4 minutes or more in the microwave with an aerated lid on.

Finely chopping and cooking vegetables means much bigger quantities can be eaten which may increase the vitamin C intake. Microwaved runner beans are first cut diagonally at 1½-inch intervals. Add 2 tbsp water and cook for about 3 minutes.

Microwave small carrots and small potatoes, for
4-6 minutes, depending on quantities, with an
aerated lid to release some steam. If they are
cooked, an inserted skewer will come out
easily.

Wicked ways with green vegetables

If you are not a natural vegetable aficionado, sprouts, cabbage and
green beans can be chopped, washed and jazzed up in many ways.
Here are five suggestions:

Method 1: Using a shallow frying pan, fry chopped vegetable
lightly in a little butter and/or oil for a minute or two before com-
pleting cooking by simmering for a few minutes in a light covering of liquid such as water, milk or wine. Serve with a good shake
of white pepper. (Good for cabbage.)

Method 2: Lightly boil for about 4-6 minutes (depending on size)
then drain well and crush and add to a frying pan of crispy
chopped bacon pieces along with crushed garlic and a final sprinkling of black pepper. Cream is an optional extra too. (Bacon,
cream and for that matter black pepper seem to 'lift' most dishes.)

Method 3: Boil lightly for a few minutes and serve with a dressing
of two parts olive oil to one part balsamic vinegar, a pinch of sugar
and a sprinkling of toasted almonds or pine nuts. (Fried onions
also may be added.)

Method 4: Boil to cook and then lightly sauté in melted butter with
chopped thyme till slightly caramelised. Garnish with lemon or
lemon zest.

Method 5: Boil then sauté as above in plain butter till caramelising
then add chestnuts and salt and pepper and warm through. The
chestnuts may be crushed lightly first if the vegetables are small.
(Optional extras are sweetcorn nibs and fried chopped bacon.)

Kale and cabbage are good when boiled for 3-4 minutes, drained
then heated through with milk (coconut milk is nice) with a small
sprinkling of curry powder or cumin and black pepper.

Spicy cabbage means stir frying finely cut fresh ginger, crushed garlic, chopped onion and seasoning for about 7 minutes till soft and golden. Next add cumin, turmeric and mustard (seeds may be used and they will pop.) Finally add chopped cabbage and a splash of water that covers and cook 5 minutes till soft. Serve instantly.

Tempura batter is excellent for vegetables. What doesn't taste better battered? (I'd draw the line at Mars bars.) Broccoli florets are perfect battered as the batter adds interest and keeps the broccoli warm much longer.

Take two raw florets per person. To make enough batter to serve 4, slowly mix 100g of plain flour with 1-2 tbsp water till it is a coating consistency. Take a saucepan and fill with enough oil to come half way up the pan.

Heat it till it is hot enough to lightly brown a cube of bread. At that point quickly dip florets in batter and quickly transfer to pan and deep fat fry till golden.

Drain well with a slotted spoon onto kitchen paper and keep warm till finished. It's a fiddly and potentially dangerous process, best done with the pan on a back burner and no distracting children (or adults) around.

Cooked vegetables or legumes as the main course

Legumes (peas, beans and lentils) are full of fibre and vitamins and form the basis of many dishes abroad. They are also a source of protein. What follows are not necessarily vegetarian dishes but dishes where the emphasis is not on meat.

Falafels: Confession: I love falafels. They have a lovely, herby fragrance and a tasty crispy exterior and soft inside. But they can be a bit of a faff to fry. (Is that where the word came from?

A proper falafel. If you fry them take care to let them set before flipping over or consider oven baking on a tray in a moderate oven (170°C) if making a lot. Variations follow but perhaps start with the classic falafel overleaf:

Egyptian falafels (makes about 7 chickpea patties)

400g tin chickpeas, rinsed & drained
a garlic clove, chopped
1 tsp ground cumin
1 tsp mild chilli
1 tsp ground coriander
(or a small handful of fresh)
small red onion, chopped
small handful flat parsley
1 tbsp olive oil for frying or greasing
baking tray

Lightly blitz chickpeas with onion, herbs and a shake of salt. If mix is too sticky you may also need 1-2 tbsp flour. If mix is too dry, you may need a little Greek yogurt or beaten egg. Rest mix for half an hour in fridge if time and it will be easier to handle.

A tablespoon of mix can be shaped into a flattened golf ball size making 6 or 7 patties. (Coat with sesame seeds if desired.) Fry about 3 minutes each side or bake for about 15-20 minutes in a moderate oven, 180°C / 160°C fan / gas 4, having oiled the baking tray first. Turn over halfway through.

Variations include: chopped dried apricots, dates, oregano, cinnamon and ginger. Another option is instead of chickpeas substitute 150g / 5oz English garden peas (fresh or defrosted) with a cooked sweet potato. Chopped spring onions may replace red ones.

Serve falafels with a juicy salad or in wraps or pitta bread with fried halloumi, crème fraiche, harissa paste and mango chutney. Pine nuts are optional.

Falafels are also good with tzatziki or hummus or a carton of yogurt mixed with the juice of half a lemon, 2 tbsp chopped coriander and a half garlic clove crushed.

Lentil burgers

Mix cooked lentils with chopped onion, garlic, ginger, cumin, coriander and chilli. They may be coated with sesame seeds or left uncoated before frying lightly for 3 minutes either side.

Feta and spinach burgers (makes eight small ones)

**1-2 tbsp olive oil for frying
1 plump red onion, finely chopped
pinch of chilli powder
125g spinach leaves, finely chopped
(frozen can be used)
110g feta, chopped small
200g tin of chickpeas, washed,
drained and mashed
75-100g breadcrumbs*
1 beaten egg
2-3 tbsp flour**

* Check consistency before adding all flour and breadcrumbs

Mix in a big bowl and try to get a stiffish consistency that can be shaped. I prefer them not to be blitzed as it's nice to see the feta pieces. Shape into about 8 patties and place on an olive oiled baking tray. Bake in the oven 20 minutes at 200°C / 180°C fan /gas 6 remembering to flip over halfway through or fry on hob 3-4 minutes each side.

Stuffed jacket potatoes

Wash and brush medium-sized potatoes and remove any eyes. Prick all over and microwave for 9 minutes for one potato. Or better still bake a few in a moderate oven 180°C / 160°C fan /gas 4 with a metal skewer inserted in each one for just over an hour until the skewer slides out easily.

Suggested fillings, as seen on most pub menus are:

• grated cheese possibly mixed with some finely chopped onion
• Coronation chicken which is cooked chicken chunks mixed with
a curry flavoured mayo and yogurt mix
• tuna mixed with mayonnaise
• prawns in a Marie Rose sauce (ketchup and mayo mixed)

Leeks wrapped in English ham (serves four)

2-3 leeks each, cut in about 4 portions (same width as the ham)
2-3 slices of ham or prosciutto
½ pint cheese sauce
salt and pepper

Wash leeks well as upper part can be gritty. No need to throw the
top green leaves away unless withered. Slice and soak leeks carefully just in case any trapped dirt remains. Lightly boil the leeks
for about 7-10 minutes till soft but not soggy. Drain and cool.
Wrap in ham and pour over cheese sauce before baking for 15-20
minutes in a moderate oven. Delicious with mash.

Leeks are the most enriching of vegetables, more mild and subtle
than onions yet pungent and fresh in aroma. They are good mixers
especially with potato and bacon and enhance most casseroles and
soups.

I was put off cooking leeks because my college cookbook stated
that they need soaking in cold water for some time to remove
trapped soil in their tops. But if you are aware of this possibility
and give them a quick rinse under the tap after they have been
sliced you can see any dirt which needs removing.

Glamorgan sausages – Selsig Morgannwg

(makes about 12 sausages)

Made from cheese and leeks, they are sausage-like in shape only
but so delicious. In this recipe the leek is cut in half lengthwise
then quartered lengthwise before slicing crosswise to get very
small pieces.

150g breadcrumbs (or skirlie stuffing: see page 49)
2 eggs
150-175g grated cheese: Caerphilly or Cheddar
1-2 tsp mustard powder
1 small leek, finely chopped*
3 tbsp milk
1 tbsp chopped parsley or thyme
a little flour may be necessary
good shake of salt and pepper

Mix together all ingredients and shape into 12 or more little sausages which are fried lightly all over till golden brown. *If you have time first sauté the chopped leek for 5 minutes in butter.

Beetroot and beef burgers (makes about 6 or more)

400g minced beef
50-75g raw, grated beetroot*
1 tsp horseradish sauce seasoning
beaten egg
12g breadcrumbs if needed
1-2 tbsp olive oil for frying

* if using cooked beetroot, chop small.

Mix all together and add seasoning. Add as many breadcrumbs as needed for a firm mix that holds together. (Optional: chill for 15 minutes.) Shape into 4-6 burgers. Fry or barbecue each side for 5-6 minutes.

Rice fritters (makes 6-8)

½ cup of cooked long-grain rice
1 onion, finely chopped and sautéed
1 tsp mustard
¼ cup plain flour
dash of nutmeg
1 egg and 2½ tbsp milk
up to 50g Cheddar cheese
oil for frying

optional: cooked prawns, chopped fine

Place rice in bowl and add cheese and onion, flour, seasoning and nutmeg. Mix mustard, milk and egg then add to rice mixture. Heat a tbsp oil in frying pan. When hot drop in a tablespoonful of rice mixture. As it sets, add another till pan is full. Fry all fritters for about 3 minutes each side till golden. Drain on kitchen paper. Keep warm till serving.

Rosti pizza

Make the base as directed on page 47 (rosti potato cakes). If your potato base is thin and crispy, it will make a tasty and healthy substitute for a pastry base pizza. (The pitta bread recipe would work well too if the dough is rolled thin for a big, crispy base.) When the potato base is baked, remove from oven and spread over a thin layer of tomato puree.

Complete with anything you fancy like cooked sliced mushrooms, tomatoes, salami, ham or chorizo slices and olives (or tuna chunks and prawns) but don't forget the anchovies, essential to any decent pizza. Anchovies always punch way above their weight. Finish with a light layer of grated cheese. Return to hot oven 200°C / 180°C fan / gas 6 until cheese is melted. Enjoy.

Alternatives to chips with everything

The British have a reputation for serving chips with everything, even sandwiches these days, and this produces a carbohydrate overload. Once upon a time when you asked for a sandwich you would be served a sandwich:
   'Can I just have a sandwich please and not the accompanying chips?' 'Of course.'
   But then the bill comes and you pay for the chips too because:
   'The till doesn't allow for individual changes. Everything is itemised, madam. Sorry.'
   'Huh.'
   Unlike the continent, few establishments here can give you what you want as opposed to the corporate diktats from Head Office. My experience of Ireland is different. Having just landed in Dublin for the first time, we started earnestly on the Guinness. 'Do

you do food?' I enquired later and received a definite, 'No.' Panic
was about to set in when the landlord later whispered in my ear in
his beautiful brogue, 'Now I've found some smoked salmon and
soda bread. Would that suit you?' Indeed, it did: the perfect part-
ner to Guinness.

Back in the UK, a whole generation has been manipulated by
set combination menus and inflexible tills to receive excessive
portions of food and drink. I love it when occasionally the man behind the bar who takes your order doesn't frown at your adapted
choice but looks at the till and says, 'Ah right. Now let me see
how I can put that through. No problem.'

The obesity crisis might be solved with more flexibility in
menus and giving choice in portion sizes. Perhaps a return to the
old 10-inch plates and 125ml wine glasses not 250ml might help.

As gastro pubs seem to be getting slightly less popular, pubs
might consider continental style tapas and mezzes as a more
relaxed and healthier accompaniment to drinking. Anyway, here
are some alternatives to chips. Not that I don't like chips. I do. But
'everything in moderation,' as my mother kept telling me.

Note: King Edward, Maris Piper and Desiree potatoes are the
best all-rounders and suit most methods of cooking. They especially make good, fluffy chips, creamy mash and crispy roasties.
Waxy new potatoes such as Jersey and Charlotte suit salads
whereas boiling or baking suits Vivaldi potatoes.

Dauphinoise potatoes (serves four)

Quick in preparation and utterly delicious, this dish may be made
in advance when entertaining or anticipating stress. It's wonder-
fully creamy and comforting and lends itself to most meat or fish
dishes. If I'm under more pressure than usual, I find it makes a
quick tea simply served with prawns and peas. Marvellous.

The cooking time can also be halved by microwaving the slices for
5 minutes before adding cream and butter and baking in a
moderate oven for 20-30 minutes.

600g potatoes (preferably waxy)
small tub single cream
optional: **crushed clove of garlic**
25g butter
salt and pepper

Oven at 190°C / 170°C fan / gas 5. Peel and thinly slice potatoes. Mop up excess starchy juice by drying slices between layers of kitchen paper or a clean tea towel if you don't mind adding to the laundry load. Oil or butter the bottom of a medium casserole and make layers of potato slices, seasoning between each layer. Finally, pour over cream. Dot the top with butter. Bake for an hour till slices are soft and the top is golden.

Sweet potatoes

Sweet potatoes contain more sugar than white ones but also more vitamins and minerals, especially vitamin A. They can be roasted, mashed, chipped or baked in the same way as white potatoes. Try sprinkling on Cajun spices, New Orleans style. It makes a change, as my mother-in-law would say when she wasn't sure about something.

I like to cook them alongside white potatoes to hedge my bets. And I totally disagree with whichever Oxbridge quiz master said he wanted to put Cajun food in his room 101 because it was derivative. He obviously doesn't get out enough if he has never heard of fusion. Derivative my foot.

Cauliflower rice

Remember that cauliflowers peak in April when they present, like I did once, a lovely, firm, creamy, youthful look. Cauliflower rice is a good way to take advantage of their prime. It is excellent served with chilli con carne and bowls of sliced avocado and yogurt or more authentically guacamole, sour cream and salsa.

Place florets in processor or blender for a short time till chopped florets resemble grains of rice. Repeat as required. Heat a little olive oil and fry 'rice' lightly for 5-10 minutes. Add salt and pepper. You need a big processor to make a lot as with a little one there's 'rice' everywhere.

Greek Oven Potatoes

When I asked a Greek waiter how long they are baked, he looked me in the eye and slowly said, 'A looong time and very, v e r y sloooowly' by which time his eyes and voice had seduced me and I'd forgotten my question.

I reckon they take about 2-3 hours in a low oven, 140°C / 120°C fan. But these Greek women don't go out much and who in Britain wants the oven on all day in summer. Enter the slow cooker. It took me a while to master and to realise that I had to do the opposite of the instructions. Now I switch it on early, having coated the cooker first with oil.

For stews and soups, first brown meat and vegetables in a frying pan and season to seal in the flavour and get food hot so it starts cooking sooner. In the case of Greek potatoes, a pale finish is desirable so place peeled potatoes in the slow cooker, preferably waxy ones and bigger than you might normally cook. Add oregano, lemon juice, olive oil and splash each potato with boiling hot water. (Cook more potatoes than you need as they come in useful and keep a few days in the fridge.) Leave to cook for at least a couple of hours whilst you write a poem, dig the garden or clean the grill pan. The great thing about the slow cooker is: you can forget it for a while.

But be warned. Though it is hard to burn things, it is not impossible. Time yourself with the poem, the garden or the grill pan.

Creamy mash potatoes

Mash is the most popular British alternative to chips and it is easy to freeze and thaw. It suits gravy dishes, particularly bangers and mash where onion gravy is made from the pan juices of the fried sausages (deglazing). Mash calls for a floury variety of potato such as Maria Piper or King Edward.

200g floury potatoes, cubed
40g butter
Splash of milk or cream
salt and ground black pepper

Boil for no more than twenty minutes till cooked and drain immediately. Mash with butter and seasoning to your taste and sufficient milk or cream to achieve a soft fluffy texture.

Throughout history potatoes have been the staple diet of Ireland. The devastating potato famine between 1845-1852 caused a million people to die and a million to emigrate thus changing the course of Irish history

Here are two ways the Irish vary their mash:

Colcannon: beat some chopped, cooked cabbage into the mash.

Champ: beat in some chopped spring onions or scallions (lovely word) as the Irish call them.

Both dishes are delicious. But nobody is going to arrest you if you add what you like to your mash (except the food snob police who don't like derivative food.) Indeed, mash is a good way of using up tasty leftovers.

White bean mash (serves two)

470g can of white beans (if fresh are
available, boil till soft)
a crushed garlic clove
zest of a lemon
a tbsp olive oil mixed with 12g melted
butter

Mash or blend it all together, adding salt and pepper. Heat through and serve garnished with rosemary. That's it! It may also double as a healthy spread or pâté for toast.

Broad bean mash

---

1 tbsp olive oil
500g fresh or frozen broad beans
3 cloves crushed garlic
a few sprigs of fresh chopped thyme
(or 1 tsp dried thyme)
a bay leaf
zest of a small lemon

Heat olive oil gently. Add 500g fresh or frozen broad beans, 2 or 3 cloves of crushed garlic, thyme, bay leaf, lemon zest and salt and pepper. Sauté 2 minutes then add enough water to cover and cook gently till it is 'reduced' which means that all the water is gone but nothing is burnt! It should be soft enough to mash. Taste and adjust seasoning if necessary and add enough olive oil to make it scrumptious. Great with bangers.

Celeriac and potato mash: Cook till soft and mash together in equal amounts.

Boiled or mashed celeriac

Peel celeriac. Chop into 1-2 cm squares. Sauté in 3 tbsp olive oil and lemon and thyme for 3-5 minutes. Cover with boiling water and simmer for 20-25 minutes, with lid off for last 10 minutes. Serve when soft or mash if preferred. (Vary by substituting lemon with crushed garlic clove.)

Butternut squash

First it might be peeled and cut into chunks. It can be roasted in a moderately hot oven (200°C) for about 40 minutes or it can be softly boiled or then mashed. It can be enjoyed plain or served with either fragments of feta or stilton and walnuts. It may be enlivened with some Greek yogurt, honey and walnuts.

Another variation: sauté a chopped onion in olive oil for a few minutes till golden and soft. Then add cubes of squash flesh and cook a minute before covering with chicken or vegetable stock. Simmer about 15 minutes. Drain and mash with a little cream.

Polenta mash

Cook polenta according to instructions. Add a little grated cheese, salt and pepper and then mash together.

Polenta chips

Unlike proper chips but they are a nice idea so I may persevere.

Bring 100ml milk and 100ml water to boil. Sprinkle on 50g polenta and cook 10 minutes stirring till thick and coming away from sides of the pan. Add 1dssp grated parmesan or cheddar and a dssp melted butter, salt and stir well. Spread polenta onto a lightly greased baking tray to form an even layer 2cm-3cm thick. Refrigerate an hour then cut polenta into chips 10cm long. Spread them out and deep fat fry for 2 minutes. Drain carefully and season.

"One cannot think well, love well, sleep well, if one has not dined well."

Virginia Woolf

Punchnep

This is a traditional Welsh recipe where boiled swede, potatoes and carrots are mashed, seasoned, then beaten together with enough butter and cream to get a puree. Some recipes call for immediate serving whilst others insist on baking at 200°C / 180°C fan / gas 6 for 20 minutes till golden and crisp.

To get the unique punchnep taste, the vegetables should be boiled in separate pans and mashed separately. However, if I'm rushed (which is always) I do it all in the same pan. It freezes well and makes a tasty and nutritious accompaniment to roast meat.

Our Welsh decorator, Tony, says he loves it as a treat for breakfast served with bacon and tomato ketchup.

Neeps and tatties are the Scottish way of mashing cooked potato with cooked swede or turnip. There is something called 'clapshot' which is similar but I wouldn't ask anyone to pass me the 'clapshot', would you?

Potato cakes

These are a great way of using up leftover mash. Add a little flour and shape into cakes and lightly fry or bake on an oiled tray till golden brown. If making a lot of cakes or to stretch out the leftover mash, add a small beaten egg and 50g flour per 150g of mash.

Potato cheesecakes

225g mash
50g SR flour with salt and pepper
85g Cheddar, grated
(or any hard cheese)
1 egg

Mix all ingredients into a pliable dough. Shape into cakes which are fried in a little olive oil for 3 or 4 minutes each side.

Rosti potato cakes (serves four)

Potato rosti is a good accompaniment to bacon and egg for brunch or meat or fish dinner dishes or may be served with salad and a yogurt dip like tzatziki for a light lunch.

2 medium large potatoes
2 tbsp flour
1 small egg, beaten
oil for frying
seasoning
variations: add some sweet potato or
cheese or a tasty mix of finely
chopped apple and beetroot.

Peel and coarsely grate potatoes. Dry between kitchen paper or a tea towel to remove excess starchy moisture. Place in a bowl. Mix with flour, seasoning and half a beaten egg. Heat a little oil in a small frying pan and add 4 or more large tbsp of potato mix, pressing flat with a wooden spoon.

Cook 5-10 minutes. When well set and brown turn over carefully with a fish slice and cook other side for same time. (Or if you make a big cake, bake in a hot oven 200°C / 180°C fan for 20 minutes.)

Frying pans that can go in the oven suit the big potato cake. Vary the size of the pan to suit the amount of potatoes which should form a half-inch layer. Rosti cakes make an excellent healthy base for a pizza too. See page 18.

Braised red cabbage

A good accompaniment to game and roast meats.

800g cabbage
¼ tsp ground cloves
¼ tsp cinnamon
400g onions
1-2 tbsp brown sugar
1-2 tbsp wine vinegar
200g cooking apples, peel, core, chop
12g butter
1 crushed or finely chopped garlic
salt and black pepper

Having removed tough outer leaves, cut into quarters and remove stalk. Rinse briefly under tap. Shred finely and season well. In a large casserole arrange layers of cabbage, garlic, spices and apples and on last layer add vinegar and butter. Add a well-fitting lid and cook for 2 - 2½ hours at 150°C. This dish reheats and freezes well. It is gorgeous with bangers and mash.

"Life is too short to stuff a mushroom."

Shirley Conran

Stuffed mushrooms

I hate to disagree with super-
woman, Shirley Conran, but
four big flat field mushrooms,
quickly wiped, stalk removed,
plonked on a baking tray,
each topped with a knob of
butter or a favourite stuffing
or cheese (blue is nice) and
baked in a hot oven 200°C /
180°C fan / gas 6 for 20
minutes make a quick, easy
and delicious accompaniment or a tasty starter.

Big button mushrooms may also be used. They are also delicious
when fried whole and served with smoked bacon in a garlic white
wine sauce or an Espagnol sauce.

An alternative stuffing:

Skirlie

A Scottish speciality using healthy oatmeal instead of highly processed flour.

> **50g suet**
> **seasoning**
> **½ tsp finely grated lemon**
> **175g stoneground medium oatmeal**
> **1 tsp mixed herbs**
> **milk to bind if softness desired**
> **optional extra: a chopped onion**

Fry all the ingredients together for 5-10 minutes. (If a crunchier
texture is required try 5 minutes at high heat to get the toasty taste.
For a softer, smoother texture add at least 2 minutes more on a
lower heat.)

(Incidentally sweet skirlie makes a great topping for desserts. For rhubarb or apple crumble replace the usual unhealthy processed flour with stoneground medium oatmeal, a little light brown caster sugar and some butter. Use twice as much oatmeal as butter: ie 100g oatmeal, 50g butter and 20g sugar would cover two dessert bowls of stewed fruit.)

Ratatouille (serves at least six)

3 tbsp olive oil
2 large onions, diced
440g tomatoes, chopped
2 red peppers, sliced
1 big aubergine, diced
1 courgette, sliced
3 garlic cloves, crushed
fresh parsley chopped

Whoever invented this deserves a medal. It's easy, nutritious, delicious and best made in advance as the flavour improves on standing. Dishes made in advance are good for the chef's nerves. Traditionally, continental vegetables are used but throw in what you fancy though the tomatoes and onions are essential. Left-over ratatouille may be used as a pizza topping. It is also tasty on toast.

Fry onion and peppers lightly for 5 minutes. Do not brown. Add aubergine and courgette and sauté a few minutes before adding tomatoes. Cover with a lid and cook for 20 minutes or longer till soft. Serve with a chopped parsley garnish.

Sensational Sauces

PURE, fresh food needs no adornment. Sauces may even destroy or distract from the true flavour. Envy the Lord and Lady of the Manor who live off their organically farmed land, enjoying the best fresh food. Yet when ingredients are sparse or inferior, a good sauce can work wonders. The French are justly proud of their sauces which they claim would make the soles of old boots taste good.

Café de Paris Sauce: a good all-rounder

Excellent with steak or crispy fresh fried fish, especially if the fish was not recently caught. Mix the following ingredients together.

> **1 cup of Madeira (or sherry)**
> **1 tbsp anchovy paste**
> **(or 3 or 4 mashed anchovies)**
> **1 tbsp chopped thyme and/or parsley**
> **juice of whole lemon**
> **1 large shallot**
> **(or half a red onion, finely chopped)**
> **3 tbsp butter**

Mix all the ingredients. It is not essential to have all of them. Optional extras are mayonnaise and/or a few drops of Worcester sauce.

Classic Gravy

According to the British, the British make the best gravy. I suspect this is true and results from our love of traditional roasts.

To make gravy

After a joint is roasted, lift it out of the roasting pan to somewhere warm and then place the roasting pan on the hob. Pour off excess fat. On a low heat, scatter over just enough plain flour to absorb the fat and stir for 2 minutes to form and cook the roux.

Slowly add water with flavourings like red wine, sherry or
Madeira, Worcester sauce and herbs and some vegetable liquor.
The liquor adds food value and contributes to the overall joined up
flavour which is the secret of a good roast dinner.

Bring to the boil stirring all the time and mop up those sticky
brown bits left behind after roasting. They are the result of a complex chemical reaction called 'the Maillard reaction' which gives
meat its distinctive gorgeous flavour. Next, get the gravy the consistency you like, slightly thicker for pork and stuffed joints.

Taste and add more wine if needed, a few chopped herbs (especially thyme) and seasoning to taste. If a deeper colour is desired,
add a dash more of either soya or Worcester sauce or gravy
browning. Gravy is a challenge as it comes towards the end of
cooking, when you want to escape the kitchen and wished you had
gone out for lunch and woe betide anyone who gets in your way at
this stage.

Vegetarian gravy (serves two-three)

1 onion, chopped
2 tsp Marmite or yeast extract
1 tbsp oil
1 tbsp Worcester sauce
1 tbsp flour
300ml (½ pint) water
optional: small glass red wine
crushed garlic clove
chopped herbs

Even if you are not vegetarian, there are times when gravy is essential to a meal but you lack the roast meat base.

Fry the onion until it is brown but not burnt. Add the flour and
cook 2 minutes or more. If using optional extras like garlic, wine
and herbs, add now.

Slowly stir in water including any vegetable liquor. Bring to boil
and simmer about 10 minutes before adding seasoning, Marmite
and soy sauce.

Simple barbecue sauce

1 onion (finely chopped)
2 tsp vinegar
1 tbsp olive oil
1 tsp Worcester sauce
2 tbsp tomato ketchup
4 tbsp water

Fry onion till soft. Add other ingredients. Season. Simmer 10 minutes.

For the real McCoy see page 80.

Sweet and sour sauce

Warm together:

1 tbsp pineapple juice
1 tbsp light brown sugar
1 tbsp tomato ketchup
1 tbsp vinegar
1 tbsp water

Peppercorn sauce (for the occasional indulgence)

1 tsp peppercorns, crushed lightly
25g butter
½ red onion or shallot, finely chopped
50ml beef stock
1 tbsp of brandy or sherry
2 tsp Worcester sauce
2 tsp mustard
30ml double cream

Sauté onion in butter till soft. Off heat stir in all ingredients, season and when ready to serve bring to boil.

Steak Diane sauce is similar to the above. Its main ingredients are cream, chopped, cooked mushrooms, brandy and Dijon mustard. Add 50g sliced mushrooms when onions are soft and sauté another minute. Proceed as above.

Plant-based sauces to replace flour-based ones

Rather than using modern processed flour these healthy sauces use natural ingredients as a thickening agent and so are better digested by the gut and better food value.

Cashew pasta sauce:

Per person:
50g (2oz) spaghetti
shake of garlic salt
50g (2oz) cashew nuts
75 ml of milk*
fresh chopped parsley

* or water for a lighter taste

Boil the pasta as directed on packet and whilst it is cooking, blitz cashew nuts with garlic salt and enough water to get a smooth sauce. Season. Drain pasta. Add sauce and parsley (or some cooked green vegetable like spinach) and heat through before serving on a hot plate.

The first time you taste the blended cashew nut sauce you think how interesting and complex it is. But it is rich, so go easy. Serve with chopped cherry tomatoes.

Sweetcorn sauce:

Blitz corn with some cream, butter or oil and flavouring of your choice such as crushed cumin seeds, crushed garlic, coriander and finely chopped red onion. Mustard is also a pleasant addition if serving with fish or ham.

Real tomato ketchup

This is simple and quick to make and smells so good. It accompanies burgers, meatballs and meatloaf well. Sauté onion in a saucepan till soft and golden brown. Add garlic and tomatoes and

simmer at least 5 minutes. If using fresh tomatoes add about
150ml water and cook longer till soft. Season. Blitz in a blender
till a smooth sauce consistency is reached. Taste and adjust flavour
if necessary.

1 onion, chopped fine
1 tbsp oil
1 clove of garlic, crushed
425g fresh (or canned) chopped
tomatoes
2 tsp chopped thyme or oregano
2tsp vinegar

Herb and walnut sauce

25g (1oz) walnuts
dash garlic salt
2 tbsp each of parsley and chives
1 tbsp of either mint, tarragon, dill or
basil
shake of black pepper
1 tbsp olive oil

Blitz all in the blender with 1-2 tsp water and more if needed to
get a smooth runny sauce. Enjoy the fragrance. Serve with pasta
like linguine with added prawns, chopped chicken, ham or bacon.
(Prawns and bacon are tasty.)

Bread sauce

Chop onion and gently simmer with a few cloves in milk for 20
minutes or so before stirring in breadcrumbs. It's the aroma of
Christmas in our house.

Apple sauce

Gently simmer peeled chunks of Bramley apple with a minimum
of sugar and water till soft. eg 2-3 tbsp sugar per apple and 50ml
water. The taste is a hundred times better than bought apple sauce.
It freezes well, has many culinary uses and when frozen thinly, it

is easy to slice or break off a chunk from the frozen whole.

Our English apples are so beautiful that it is a crime how often they are left to languish on the branch. One cold winter in York-shire when our second baby was new-born we looked out onto an unpicked apple tree. That the apples were regularly visited by a fieldfare made us very happy. I can still see the image now.

Cranberry sauce:

Wash cranberries. Place in saucepan. Cover quite liberally with sugar. Sprinkle with water. Simmer till soft, stirring often.

Raspberry or strawberry sauce:

Just liquidise (or mash) with sugar. Pour over poached fruit or ice cream.

Butterscotch sauce

Melted butter mixed with brown sugar and/or syrup and finally cream.

Fish, Fish, Glorious Fish

"This sceptred isle . . .
this precious stone set in the silver sea."

Shakespeare's Henry V

SLIMY, smelly, and other-worldly looking. Such was my view of fish as a child. All this despite my brother walking me up and down the silver streams of North Wales to indicate fish under rocks and eels which he carried live back to the caravan for Mum to cook for breakfast.

What a fool I was. I wish I'd tried those eels now that they are rare. One evening an eel got lost in the caravan. Every nook and cranny was searched and soon the light was fading. I was terrified. How could I sleep with a wriggling, writhing, wet sea snake on the loose. It might settle anywhere. Darkness fell, the search was abandoned.

With the aunties at the caravan and mum and dad on the ends.
Llanddulas, 1960.

Mum returned to the sink and to washing a tea towel. She reached under the sink for her packet of detergent and there in the packet was the elusive eel, blowing bubbles. It had sailed down the sink pipe and through the hole at the top of the packet on its last journey of freedom. What a relief.

Today, many people seem as frightened of fish as I was then. Our UK consumption is less than a third of Japan and a fifth of Norway.

Some supermarket staff cannot tell a herring from a kipper without reading the label and our best catch of lobsters, prawns and crabs is often sold abroad where it is most appreciated.

My fear of fish was overcome when I became a diver and enjoyed swimming amongst fishes and sharing their peaceful, beautiful habitat. I then appreciated their iridescent beauty and the amazing taste of fresh fish.

Seafood for Breakfast

Kippers (or herrings) are a good source of vitamin D and make a stunning start to the day and take seconds to heat up. If you worry about ending up in A&E with a bone stuck in your throat buy filleted fish or use your fingers to eat it, having first removed the big back bone which should come away in one go. OK. It's a fiddle, but worth it. Have a go! (Left to myself I would use my fingers to eat everything, except soup of course.)

Welsh laver cakes make a tasty addition to egg and bacon and are pleasingly quick and easy to make. Should you stray onto a Welsh beach and see ladies in shawls and tall black hats gathered round rocks collecting something in their baskets, it's laverbread seaweed.

Fortunately for us, we can buy *Parsons' tins of laverbread* from speciality shops or on the internet saving hours of preparation.

Welsh laver cakes

120g tinned laverbread
30g medium or fine oatmeal
(porridge oats)

Mix the laverbread and oatmeal to a firm consistency and shape into little cakes 2-inch diameter and ½-inch thick. Fry carefully for about 3 minutes on each side with bacon rashers. Keeping them in shape is a skill which comes with practice. Laver cakes are deliciously different with a pure fresh taste of the sea.

Breakfast prawns

Some home pleasures must be forsaken when travelling abroad even to Greece, where according to my husband the bacon is awful. I'm too busy eating fresh fruit and yogurt to worry but in the Peloponnese village of Stoupa, we once shared a delicious breakfast of prawns wrapped in bacon served on a terrace overlooking a shimmering turquoise sea.

The tavernas were old Venetian houses, complete with peeling paint on fading elegant doors. 'Shabby chic' was no doubt invented by the Greeks. Watching the sunlight dance on the turquoise waves whilst eating those succulent prawns was the best start possible to a day.

Per person: 2-3 jumbo prawns and 2-3 streaky bacon (known as 'angels on horseback' when enclosing oysters or 'devils on horseback' when enclosing prunes. The 'devils' would also make a good breakfast.)

Stretch each bacon rasher with a rolling pin: bash or roll. Trim the rasher to same width as the prawn and wrap tightly. Fry or grill till crisp turning over once. Serve with fresh fruit juice and find somewhere nice to eat it.

Note: Wrapping in bacon improves many foods: most obviously sausages. Dried apricots are especially delicious wrapped in a rasher of bacon which has been pressed flat.

For a party, you get a number of canapés on a baking tray and cook at 200°c for about 20 minutes. Turn down and keep warm.

(Thank you Lesley for this recipe. They smelt and tasted gorgeous, especially on that warm summer evening in your colourful garden.)

Cooking Fresh Fish

If your fish has just been caught, and this is where camping by water comes into its own, take a sharp knife and scrape off scales if there are any, then cut off the head and tail. Next, preferably with scissors, cut open the under belly side. Scrape out entrails.

Wash fish inside and out and dry with kitchen paper. (It is optional whether to remove the backbone by pressing fish flat to loosen it first. Often people just remove flesh from bone when eating.)

Finally melt a little oil or butter and allow fish to kiss frying pan on both sides till golden. If you have them handy, garnish with fresh parsley and serve with chunks of lemon, fat enough to squeeze lemon juice over your fabulous tasting fresh fish.

Michael lands a catch. Aberdaron, 1986.

Whole baked salmon

What's nicer than arriving at a dining table to see a platter of whole salmon waiting for you (thank you Caroline) accompanied by a simple summer salad and new potatoes. With or without the head on, this fish looks impressive when served whole, accompanied by a jug of Hollandaise or dill sauce or wild garlic mayo.

some parsley sprigs
thickly-sliced lemon, sliced
generous sheet of foil to enclose fish
bay leaf
whole gutted salmon 4-6lb
½ glass white wine

Place middle of sheet of foil on roasting tray and brush with oil or butter. Place salmon on sheet and stuff parsley, lemon and bay leaf in cavity. Splash with wine and seal foil to cover fish with a loose fit to allow air circulation but make sure edges are well sealed all round by folding over a few times. Bake at 190°C / 170°C fan / gas 5. Check after 40-50 minutes. It may take 10 minutes more.

Test with skewer inserted into deepest bit for 10 seconds. The flesh should look opaque and the skewer should feel warm when removed. Gently remove skin whilst fish is warm.

Scottish smoked haddock (serves two)

Smoked haddock fillet was the only fish I would eat as a child because it didn't look like a fish and there was no bother with bones. I enjoyed something similar to this particular version in the splendour of The Dome restaurant, Edinburgh. It can be served with cooked neeps and tatties, mash or boiled potato slices crisped up in the oven.

300g smoked haddock, skinned
200ml milk
1 tbsp cornflour
75g grated cheese
salt and ground pepper
1 tsp mustard
1 thickly sliced and washed leek
diced ham or cooked bacon
2 cooked medium potatoes, keep warm

Simmer big chunks of leeks in a saucepan for about 10 minutes till tender. Remove leeks to a warm place but keep liquor in pan. Place haddock in a shallow frying pan of suitable size. Cover fish with milk and simmer a few minutes till just opaque. Keep 'fish milk' but remove fish to a warm place.

Blend cornflour with a little milk. Put fish liquor with leek liquor in a saucepan. Add cornflour that has been blended with 1 tbsp water. Slowly bring to boil, stirring all the time. It should be a slightly runny coating sauce so add more fish and vegetable liquor if needed.

Off heat, add grated cheese, mustard and seasoning. Again, adjust consistency, possibly with a dash of white wine. Put fish in the middle of each plate and encircle with leeks and potatoes. Pour hot sauce over, mainly on the fish in the middle. Serve with a sprinkle of diced ham or cooked bacon on top.

Sole (or any white fish fillet) with salsa verde (serves two)

This salsa has an amazing sharp but delicious taste which enhances plain fish perfectly. It is quick and easy to make and smells so healthy whilst you're making it.

Salsa verde:	**small handful each of flat parsley and basil, finely chopped**
	1 dssp cider vinegar
	50ml olive oil
	1 dssp capers
	½ - 1 tsp Dijon mustard
optional:	**1 clove garlic, crushed**
	2 soles or any white fish fillet
	25g butter
	dssp oil for frying

First blitz the salsa ingredients in a blender till smooth. Fry fish fillets in butter till opaque and serve with salsa verde. Capers go well with most fish especially smoked salmon.

Mackerel

It is important that the mackerel is very fresh as its unique, subtle flavour soon deteriorates. Ideally, catch the fish yourself and cook it immediately. Not so long ago, mackerel could be caught as soon as you threw the hook in but has anyone noticed that there are fewer fish in the sea? Not to mention more people on the land.

Mackerel is often paired with gooseberries. They are in season at the same time. I prefer this salsa to the sauce as the sharpness of the salsa counteracts the richness of the mackerel. If fresh fruit is not available, tinned fruit will do fine.

An admission ahead of the next recipe: I don't grill fish. In fact I haven't grilled anything ever since we had to call the fire brigade when daughter left a goat's cheese tart under the grill. Husband was in the bath relaxing. Smoke was everywhere. I called the fire brigade then son arrived and sorted it. Once called the fire brigade do not go back.

Now I prefer to use a hot, barely oiled frying pan which I watch carefully. If you use olive oil I suspect it is as healthy as grilling. Fatty grill pans catching fire and a kitchen full of smoke are a thing of the past. Quite boring really, especially as the firemen were so nice.

Mackerel with gooseberry salsa

Run the sharp edge of a big knife over body to remove scales. Cut off tail and then head below gills and pull out guts. Rinse the inside with water, checking all guts removed. You can cook it like this. (If it is a big fish it may be filleted by slitting underside open and pressing hard on skin side to flatten and open, then turn over and carefully lift out the back bone.) Fry or grill both sides till crispy. Serve with salsa or sauce.

Salsa:

> **150g gooseberries, topped and tailed**
> **salt and pepper**
> **tbsp each vinegar and sugar**
> **half an onion, finely chopped**
> **zest and juice from lime or lemon**

Add gooseberries to a splash of water with a tbsp vinegar and a tbsp sugar, salt and pepper and simmer a minute or two then rest (the gooseberries, not you). Add 1 tsp chopped chives and 1 tbsp chopped parsley and lemon or lime juice and zest. Chill for 3 hours.

Gooseberry Sauce: Melt 20g butter and add 200g washed, topped and tailed gooseberries. Splash with water and gently cook about 20 minutes till soft. Add 1tsp sugar, a shake of salt and pepper and 50g cream.

Mackerel baked in cider (serves two)

Baking is easy and may make use of heat if a moderate oven is on anyway. This dish can also be cooked 'en papillote': wrap the fish in foil after sprinkling with cider or wine.

2 fillets of mackerel
25g butter
50g stewed gooseberries
wine glass of cider

Lay two fillets in an oiled or buttered dish and season and dot with butter. Cover with topped and tailed gooseberries and pour over a large wine glass of dry cider.

Bake in a moderate oven 170°C / 150-160°C fan for 20 minutes. Serve with juices.

Whitebait

Can be lightly coated in either flour or cornflour or an equal mix. I use cornflour with some added black pepper. Shallow fry for two or more minutes. They often stick together which makes it easy to lift them up and turn over.

Fry the other side for 2-3 minutes. Drain off fat with kitchen paper. Serve with fat wedges of lemon. Not only do you have the intrinsic flavour but also memories of purple-pink Mediterranean sunsets and the caress of the warm, scented breeze which ruffles a pearlescent sea. Somehow a can of sardines can't do this.

"I can find some whitebait and Pelagia can flour
them and fry them in oil
and squeeze lemon juice all over them."

Louis de Bernières' Captain Corelli's Mandolin

Tapas

Silver-filleted anchovies in olive oil are a favourite abroad and
most big supermarkets sell them here. In Spain anchovies, sardines
and prawns are a tapas treat alongside other delicacies like Spanish
omelette, stuffed mushroom or tomatoes, asparagus, chorizo and
meatballs in tomato or almond sauce and of course olives.

Tavernas such as Marineras, opposite the harbour in Fuengirola,
have a tapas counter for customers to select from. In some Spanish
restaurants tapas appears to be morsels of left-over main dishes
and very delicious they are. I wish tapas would catch on over here.

Popular Fish Dishes

Seafood Tart (serves four)

This dainty, delicious dish pleases most fussy fish eaters. Any left-
over fish works but this combination is very tasty.

	150ml milk*
	1 tbsp laverbread (supermarkets sell tinned)
	150ml single cream*
	6 rashers <u>cooked</u> smoked diced bacon
	2 large eggs*
	90g cockles (if pickled, steep in water an hour. Rinse. Drain.)
	100g Caerphilly (or any hard cheese)*
	100g cooked cold water prawns
	salt and pepper
For the short pastry:	**75g butter**
	150g plain flour
	pinch of salt, enough water to bind

*300ml left-over cheese sauce can replace these ingredients.

Short pastry: rub 75g butter into 150g plain flour with a pinch of salt and just enough water to bind. (See Appendix, page 192).

Filling: Line an 8-inch (21cm) flan tin with baking paper and then pastry. Bake blind for 5 minutes at 200°C / 180°C fan / gas 6. (Baking beans over greaseproof paper stops the pastry rising.) Remove and cool flan case. Reduce oven temperature to 180°C / 160°C fan / gas 4. Mix dairy products in a bowl. Add fish and all else. Mix well. Season.

Place in flan case and bake for 20-25 minutes until tart is golden and looks set or is firm in middle when cut with a sharp knife.

Simple Fish Cakes

Mix mash potato or mashed cooked chickpeas with flaked leftover fish and combine. No messy time-consuming coating is needed. Season and shape into patties. Fry cakes on both sides till crispy brown.

Rice Fish Cakes

150g cold cooked rice
2 tsp English mustard
1 small onion, finely chopped
2 tbsp milk
60g Cheddar, grated
1 egg
25g flour
1-2 tbsp oil
50g cooked prawns, chopped
(or any leftover fish, finely chopped)
seasoning

Add flavouring of choice: chopped chives, tarragon or caraway seeds or capers and ketchup. Mix mustard, milk and egg before combining with all the rest. Spoon heaped tablespoons on to hot oil and fry a few minutes on each side till golden. This is a superb way of using up left-over rice. A tad fiddly but these fish cakes are the best.

Kedgeree (serves four)

Perfect for supper or a great breakfast dish if the family chef rises early. No doubt that was not a problem at the time of the Raj from where the dish originates.

Remember that fish tastes best when slightly under-cooked. It will continue cooking on a hot plate so stop the cooking process as soon as the flesh begins to turn opaque. Peas may be included as an optional extra.

> **500g naturally smoked haddock**
> **250g rice**
> **200ml milk**
> **½ onion, finely chopped**
> **25g butter**
> **½ - 1 tsp curry powder**
> **1 crushed cardamom pod**
> **handful of chopped chives**
> **or parsley garnish**
> **1 lemon, quartered**
> **1-2 boiled eggs**

Boil rice as directed. Poach fish in milk for about 8-10 minutes before skinning and flaking. Sauté onion in butter a few minutes till soft. Add cardamom seeds and curry powder. Cook a further 2 minutes till golden brown. Add cooked seasoned rice then fish. Heat through with left-over milk. Reduce liquid and serve with quartered soft boiled eggs on top and herbs.

Paella (serves two)

This is a great dish for entertaining. It looks gorgeous if served in the paella pan in which it is cooked and dotted with prawns and mussels cooked with shells on. Some areas of Spain use meat, some fish and others both. Like risotto, you are essentially using the stock to cook rice and timing the complete evaporation of the

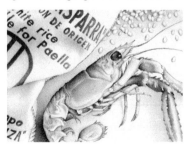

water for the end and adding other ingredients at the appropriate
time for them to cook (or heat through.)

                    1 tbsp olive oil
                    80-100g rice
                    ½ chopped onion
                    garlic clove, crushed
                    100g cooked prawns, mussels or
                    cooked sausages or chorizo
                    1 tsp dried thyme and paprika
                    40g frozen or fresh peas
    optional: **sliced pepper**
                    100g fresh chicken chunks
                    or fresh fish chunks
                    300ml chicken stock
                    4 small tomatoes
                    ½ - 1 pepper, chopped
                    seasoning
                    shake of turmeric / saffron to colour

Sauté onion and chicken or fish chunks in oil till golden brown.
Remove fish. Add rice, garlic and peppers and sauté 2 minutes
then add herbs and tomatoes. Finally add stock to simmer and
cook rice. When simmering, add peas. Keep an eye that rice has
sufficient water to cook. Be ready to top up.

Four minutes towards end, add mussels in shells (see preparation
on page 69 opposite) and raw prawns if using. When rice is
cooked and all liquid gone, quickly heat through any desired
'cooked extras' if using chorizo or cooked prawns, cooked sausage
or fish chunks cooked earlier. Wow! Harder to describe than do.
I'm going for a lie down.

> "Governing a great nation is like cooking a small
> fish – too much handling will spoil it."
>
> *Lao Tzu, Ancient Chinese philosopher*

Mussels

Mussels can be seen clinging to the anchors and ropes (or is it sheets?) of boats in harbours. Tasty and easy to cook, they are supplied from clean waters today making them safe to eat. The pale mussels are female and the bright orange ones are male.

Plain mussels (serves two)

2lb mussels
half inch of water in large frying pan

Rinse the mussels in cold running water. Pull off any beards or dirt and scrub shells. Discard broken mussels. Bring the closed whole mussels to boil in the pan. Leave to steam for 4-5 minutes. Discard any mussels which haven't opened. Alone, they are delicious or with linguine and a thin sauce like white wine garlic sauce.

What is lovely about a plate of mussels for a meal is that no other food seems necessary. People seem to find them complete.

Moules marinière (serves two-three)

800g mussels
300ml white wine
1 tbsp olive oil
salt and pepper
bay leaf
small onion, chopped
3 tbsp finely chopped parsley

Prepare mussels as above. Then fry chopped onions and garlic in large frying pan gently for about 6-8 minutes. Toss in the mussels in the shells with the white wine, black pepper and bay leaf. Bring

to boil, cover and cook 3-5 minutes. Strain liquid. Transfer mussels to warm dish discarding broken or unopened ones. Bring liquor to boil for a few minutes. Thicken if desired. Stir in parsley. Pour over mussels. Serve at once.

Greek fish stew

300g mix of 2 or 3 favourite fish
50g dry white wine
1 small onion, chopped
a few sprigs of chopped parsley and fennel
1 garlic clove, crushed
juice of a lemon
250g tomatoes, peeled and chopped
1 tbsp olive oil
pinch of sea salt
good shake of black pepper

Heat olive oil and cook finely chopped onion and garlic about 5 minutes till soft and translucent. Add fresh tomatoes, wine and water and cook for about 8 minutes till tomatoes are soft. Add fish and cook over a medium heat for 5 minutes till just opaque. Remove from heat and stir in parsley or fennel and serve with chunks of lemon.

Fish pie (serves three-four)

400g mix of any fish you like eg cod loin, smoked haddock, salmon or smoked salmon and prawns.
300g potatoes for vegetable topping of mash or boiled slices of potato (or use 200g of pastry)

300ml of milk
50-70g cheese, grated
2 tsp cornflour
small glass of white wine
seasoning

optional: small crushed garlic clove

Poach the fish in a frying pan with enough milk to cover. Simmer till nearly opaque. Remove fish. Using the same pan with fish juices in, pour in rest of milk. Make a white sauce by first warming milk. Then bring to boil and either thicken with cornflour blended with wine, stirring hard, and bring to the boil again. Or, just sprinkle two tbsp rice flour over hot milk and stir well for a minute or two.

Off the heat add cheese and adjust thickness if necessary. Stir in some sweetcorn or peas or any chopped vegetable. If mix is too thick, thin with milk. Add cooked fish. Topping could be mashed potato, cooked potato slices or puff pastry. Bake at 200°C / 180°C fan / gas 6 for 20 minutes. Garnish with parsley or chopped chives and a few cooked prawns if available.

Gourmet Sea Food

Killing lobsters and crabs was an easy matter in the old days: you plunged them into boiling, salted water for twenty minutes with a nod of a few minutes either way for a big or small beast.

In the 1970s a theory went round that it was kinder to place lobsters in a pan of cold water brought slowly to the boil to anaesthetise the lobster.

Never having cooked lobster, it was probably foolish of me to try this technique, especially when my camping pan was small. As I brought the water to the boil, the lobster, understandably, tried to climb out of its warm watery grave though I kept pushing it back in.

The sight of its blue front claws trying to escape whilst its back turned red is engraved on my conscience. From then on I have plunged lobsters into boiling water and used a big pan. Just recently it has been suggested to me that chilling the lobster with ice prior to the plunge is best. Hmm.

After cooking carefully, remove lobster from pan. When cool, break off all the claws by twisting and pulling. Take hold of the body and pull away from the tail. The white meat from the body is then easy to extract whereas the legs need hitting with a hammer or rolling pin to cause cracks so the shell can be peeled off.

A skewer helps to extract all the meat. I knew a rich lady in our diving club, June, who had a silver lobster hook for this purpose. I expect she had a silver cow creamer too and a silver champagne stopper and a set of leather backed PG Wodehouse books. I would if I was her.

Caravan and lobsters. The culinary spin-offs from deep-sea diving.
Aberdaron, 1976.

Lobster Thermidor

This simple dish is composed of lobster meat with a light cheese sauce enhanced with white wine:

- Carefully grab your live lobster's body from behind keeping fingers well away from secateur claws and plunge it into boiling water for 20 minutes. As detailed above.
- Sort meat into roughly equal bite-size portions
- Make cheese sauce, see page 75, and stir lobster meat into it.

When ready to serve, sprinkle on breadcrumbs and grill till brown in a moderate oven 180°C / 160°C fan for no more than twenty minutes. Check with a skewer inserted in middle that it is hot. It looks lovely served in the shell but a shallow casserole may be more convenient. Serve immediately with hot vegetables, rice or salad and a good Chablis.

Hawaiian Lobster (serves two)

1 tbsp olive oil
1 onion chopped fine
1 red pepper deseeded, sliced thinly
1 stick of celery, sliced thinly
third of a fresh pineapple, chunked
100g basmati rice, rinsed first
300ml fish or chicken stock
pinch of cumin or curry powder
200g lobster meat, cut into chunks
sprinkling of sultanas

Heat oil and fry onion till soft. Add pepper and celery and cook for 2 minutes before adding rice and stirring it for 1 minute. Add stock, sultanas and salt and pepper and simmer on a low heat for 20 minutes.

Check it regularly to ensure there is sufficient liquid, adding more water or white wine as desired. When the rice is soft, add lobster meat and heat through. Serve garnished with parsley.

Crab

Warning: the front pincer claws are as sharp and strong as secateurs. Keep your fingers out of reach by handling from behind the fish and grabbing its shell with both hands. If a crab can be held in one hand across its shell, it is too small to take out of the sea. Crabs should be allowed to mature and reproduce to supply nature's treasure. Many crabs landed and sold today look small enough to break regulations.

Preparing the cooked crab: some people just crack open the two big front claws for the lovely white meat and throw the legs away. That's a shameful waste. There's some good meat in the legs if you are prepared to fiddle. Twist each claw and leg to separate it from the body and access the meat by cracking with a hammer or rolling pin and removing the shell. A skewer helps to get it all out. Lucky the lady with the silver crab hook.

The instructions for preparing the main body seem difficult but soon become easy with practice and the reward is divine.

Method:
Place the crab underside up in front of you with the eyes furthest
away and the tail nearest you. Note, the female crab has a wide,
heart-shaped tail. Tap along the inside line on the underside of the
body until it is weak enough to give way under pressure and by
pressing the tail up with the thumbs it will break free from the
outer shell. Lift out the inner body framework.

Remove and discard the transparent stomach bag under the head
and the gills, often known as 'dead man's fingers' which look
grey, feathery and unappetising. Scoop out all the meat that looks
tasty and enjoy in sandwiches or salad.

(If the crab is wet inside, it was probably changing its shell which
crabs do every year. Consider using a very watery crab for fish
stock instead.)

Dressed crab (serves two)

Take a cooked medium-sized crab as they have proportionately
more tender meat. Separate the brown and white meat. Mix in a
little pepper, salt and lemon juice to the brown meat and a little
mayonnaise or French dressing or salad cream to the white meat if
you think it needs it.

Wash and dry shell and pack meat back with white in middle and
brown at each side. The contrast of white and brown meat may be
defined with a line each side of chopped parsley and paprika.
Serve with green salad.

Crab linguine

200g (8oz) fresh or thawed crab meat
150-200g linguine (thin spaghetti)

Make a light cheese sauce:

½ pint milk
25g plain flour
25g margarine or butter
50g hard cheese (grated)

A quick, easy and elegant summer lunch:

Boil the pasta as directed and make a roux sauce by melting the
fat, stirring in the flour to absorb it till it is a roux ball which
should be cooked for a couple of minutes.

Then slowly add half the milk stirring all the time on a low heat.
As it thickens gradually add the rest of the milk and bring to boil,
stirring and cooking on a low heat for a minute whilst adding salt
and pepper.

Add crab meat and heat through off the boil a few minutes. Some
white wine may be added. Drain the pasta onto a warmed plate
and pour the sauce over. Garnish with chopped dill, parsley or
fennel. That's good.

Scallops

I will never forget the first time we ate these. It was in a tent on a
diving holiday in Oban when my husband returned with them.
Having no idea how to cook them, I asked fellow divers. 'Boil in
water till the shells open and remove the white fleshy pads of
meat. My wife batters them.'
    I only had butter so I fried them in that. We took a bite, looked
at each other and thought we had gone to heaven. At home my
'Larousse Gastronomique,' said that the best way to cook scallops
is to simply fry them in butter. Aah!

Fried scallops (serves two)

Allow 6 scallops per person
50g unsalted butter

Boil the shells till they open and then remove the scallops of white flesh. Fry them gently in butter till they are opaque. Enjoy alone or serve with something bland that doesn't distract from their fabulous flavour like rice, chips or vegetables.

Squid (Calamari)

This is a peculiar-looking but tasty fish, especially peculiar if you see it swimming underwater as I did in the lovely cove of Fakari, Rhodes, where it looked like a small, folded umbrella with a large eye. Its popularity has crossed the Channel and now British squid is available here.

It is commonly eaten cut into rings and battered or even simply fried without batter. As always, fresh beats frozen. Very fresh beats everything.

one squid, prepared and cleaned
50g flour
a tbsp white wine
wine glass of water

Cut body into rings less than ¼-inch thick. Make tempura batter by putting flour in a bowl and wine and water in a well in the middle. Heat oil until it browns a cube of bread in 10 seconds. Fry battered rings in the hot oil till golden brown.

Lift out with a slotted metal spoon and drain on kitchen paper. Serve with lemon, a simple salad and perhaps a few homemade chips. Divine.

*

When I revisited Fakari in 2017, it was a messed-up building site and I cried.

Diving off Skorpios, the island home of Onassis. July 1997.

Octopus

If you catch an octopus, as someone in our diving club once did in Anglesey, place it on different coloured backgrounds and wait for Nature's magic to work as it changes colour. Then you might put it back in the sea or kill it. (I have no idea how to kill it and do not wish to know.) To prepare for eating, tenderise it. Not by singing sweet nothings to it. Quite the opposite.

Bash it against a rock till it tears easily. It can also be hung up on a washing line. (I think this is why the Greeks do this.) Or you could just cook it slowly in a casserole, having simmered it for 35 minutes first. Octopus makes a terrific casserole with tomatoes, baby onions, herbs and wine.

We first ate this in a little taverna on the Greek island of Telendos one warm, moonlit night. The evening would have been perfect had it not been for a loud American woman on the next table relating her experience with a psychotherapist. Fortunately, there was no gun around or there might have been a Greek tragedy.

Octopus casserole (serves two)

A current theory on tenderising a fresh octopus is to put it into the freezer for 24 hours then slowly thaw in the fridge. This has the merit that if you suddenly acquire an octopus you can freeze it whilst you think how to cook it. Morrisons supplied me with a cleaned octopus by special request and for only £2.86 for half a kilo.

Place it in large pan with 3 litres water and 1 tbsp vinegar. Bring to boil and simmer 30-35 minutes. Remove octopus, cool and cut into chunks. Test for tenderness. If satisfied, proceed to next stage:

1-2 tbsp olive oil
2 garlic cloves, crushed
2 tsp paprika
1 large onion, chopped
400g tomatoes
a bay leaf
1 tbsp each of oregano and thyme
third of a cup Kalamata olives, pitted
glass of red wine

Heat oil and sauté garlic and fennel 3-4 minutes. Add tomatoes, octopus chunks, wine, herbs, olives and some black pepper. Simmer for 40 minutes, adding small tender octopus chunks in last 20 minutes or earlier if still a bit chewy. Meanwhile lie back and think of Greece or perhaps you are in Greece. In your own villa. Oooh.

Note: cold cooked octopus is lovely in salads and with coleslaw and a light Marie Rose sauce.

Classic Rice Dishes

PILAU, jambalaya, gumbo, paella and risotto are all delicious rice dishes. What's the difference?

Pilau (Pilaf) is a tasty alternative to boiled rice in Indian cuisine. The raw rice is sautéed in butter first, possibly along with chopped onions and then boiled in seasoned stock to which some combination of the following may be added: garlic, vegetables like peas or chopped cabbage, dried fruit, nuts, cinnamon, cloves, saffron or cardamom, but not all of them at once. Just flaked almonds and a few gorgeously fragrant crushed Cardamom seeds are my favourite. Pilau makes a good accompaniment to white fish dishes as well as curries. See 'Nutty Pilau' on page 85.

Jambalaya (serves two-three)

Like everything in New Orleans, jambalaya is free and easy about its origin. It mixes long grain rice boiled in stock with cooked chopped onions, tomatoes and chorizo and brown shrimps. You may also add chicken or any fish or vegetables. Like paella it is a complete dish. It fuses Spanish, French and African cuisine and has no inhibitions about whether it is meat or fish based or both.

> **30g butter**
> **1 onion, chopped**
> **1 tsp salt and ½ tsp black pepper**
> **1 green pepper, chopped**
> **½ tsp thyme**
> **pinch cayenne pepper**
> **crushed bay leaf**
> **2 sticks celery, chopped**
> **2 cups chicken stock**
> **2 cloves garlic, pressed**
> **1 cup rice**
> **5 or 6 tomatoes, chopped**
> **200g mix of cooked shrimps**
> **or prawns, ham or chorizo**

Sauté the vegetables in butter till soft. Mix in tomatoes then stock and spices. Add rice and simmer for 20 minutes. Mix in cooked meat and fish and heat through for 5 minutes. Serve with chopped parsley if desired. (If you don't have an American measuring cup, check its measuring capacity on page 189.)

Gumbo, Louisiana's state dish, is a stew, served usually with a separate dish of boiled white rice. It may also take the form of a thick soup. Classic gumbo requires a strong, rich flavour which results from long, slow cooking in a rich stock and vegetables: the Louisiana Holy Trinity of onions, celery and green peppers plus optional okra and tomatoes.

The meat may be chicken, rabbit, sausages and/or sea food like brown shrimps or prawns. Worcester sauce and different spices may be used like the Cajun spices of paprika, chilli, cumin and basil or those shown here. Not too much restraint is needed for a full New Orleans flavour.

25g butter
1-2 cups chicken stock
1 large onion, chopped
1 tsp salt
1 clove garlic, crushed
½ tsp ground pepper
1 green pepper, chopped
¼ tsp each of:
cayenne pepper, chilli powder, thyme
2 celery sticks, chopped
½ crushed bay leaf
200g okra, sliced fresh or frozen
200g fresh, cooked or canned crab
400g shrimps (or prawns)
6 chopped tomatoes, peeled
100g diced cooked ham or chorizo

Sauté onion, garlic, pepper and celery till soft. Add okra and tomatoes and all other ingredients except fish or meat. Mix. Cover and simmer slowly for up to two or more hours. Five minutes before serving add cooked fish and meat and heat through well. Serve as a thick soup or with rice.

Risotto is a north Italian dish which is relatively quick to make. It is often of a creamy texture which results from using Italian Arborio pudding rice and tender meat or fish. To aid the creamy texture a soft goat's cheese (or grated hard cheese) may be stirred in or added when serving.

Welcome is the dish that is cooked and served in one pan. Some non-stick frying pans can be put into an oven and heated up to 200°c which is very useful. Risottos can be made to suit all tastes. The traditional Arborio, pudding rice, being stickier suits the substitution of green vegetables with butternut squash and/or beetroot and a soft cheese like goats cheese added at the end. I prefer to use basmati rice for a fluffier result. The skill in making risotto is ensuring that the pan does not boil dry yet the water has just evaporated before serving.

Butternut squash risotto (serves four)

flesh of a butternut squash
4 slices of bacon, finely chopped
1 leek finely sliced and washed
210g short grained rice (like Arborio)
2 garlic cloves, crushed
2 tbsp olive oil and a little butter
1 glass white wine
salt and pepper
950ml chicken stock

Peel squash. It may be easier to handle if it is cut in two first. Cube and simmer squash 20 minutes till tender. Drain. Mash or puree. Heat oil and butter in large frying pan and sauté leeks with garlic for about 4 or 5 minutes then add bacon and fry 2 minutes before adding rice. Mix and fry all this for 2-3 minutes. Add stock and wine and cook for about 20 minutes till absorbed. Take care it does not boil dry. Finally add squash and heat through. Season and serve.

Bacon and mushroom risotto (serves four)

	12g butter and a tbsp olive oil
	1 onion, chopped
	4 rashers bacon, finely chopped
	100g sliced fresh mushrooms
	150g-200g basmati or patna rice
	½ cup frozen peas
	(or other green vegetable)
	1 pint chicken stock
optional:	4-6 fresh tomatoes or small can

Gently sauté onion till soft. Add chopped bacon and mushrooms and lightly fry for about 3 minutes. Add rice and fry for a minute then add chicken stock. Boil, then simmer and add tomatoes, if using, and any other vegetable you fancy and salt and pepper.

Check it doesn't boil dry by stirring from time to time and topping up with water if needed. The trick is to only allow the water level to disappear just before serving. It should take about 15-25 minutes to cook rice. (Check packet.) Serve with a bowl of grated cheese to hand.

Paella is a traditional Spanish dish using shorter grained rice like Bomba or Calasparra which is grown in Spain, but it works with most types of rice. It uses similar ingredients to jambalaya though more restrained in flavour.

A paella pan is a good investment especially if it can go on the hob, in the oven and then on the table. Paella is excellent for entertaining, with its colourful ingredients of red peppers, green peas, pink prawns and orange mussels in blue pearly shells in yellow rice. It is easy to eat, serve and make. What more can you ask? See page 67.

Nuts for dinner

LADIES and gentlemen, I present the truly heroic, versatile, delicious and delectable, once forgotten ingredient of the culinary world: nuts. Available to you in subtle or strong flavours, hard or soft textures, to be chopped, roasted, salted or ground for a multitude of uses. You can decorate your cakes and puddings, garnish your savoury dishes and even use nuts to thicken stews and sauces.

But now (drum roll) nuts are even the star ingredient of the main dish itself. Once upon a time nuts were bought by us British only at Christmas. In a red net bag you would find unshelled Brazils, walnuts, almonds and hazelnuts, all requiring father's strength and skill with the nut crackers. Too often, the fate of these nuts was to gather dust on the sideboard beside the sherry before finding their way to the bin with the poinsettia and the half empty box of dates.

As more varieties of nuts became available, they transitioned into a pass round party dish. Today's nuts no longer play a minor role as an occasional nibble. Their versatile culinary merit along with their high nutritional value, especially protein, has established them as a rival to meat and fish. A look at any European menu will show you that it was ever thus abroad. We are the ones who seem to lose touch with nature.

Nut loaf (serves two-three)

1 sliced parsnip, boiled and cubed
1 small beaten egg
75g hazelnuts, dry fried then chopped
75g mushrooms, chopped
50g chestnuts, chopped
50g Stilton or hard cheese, crumbled or grated
1 small onion, finely chopped
20g butter
1 tbsp fresh thyme leaves
or 2 tsp dried 50g breadcrumbs, white or brown
seasoning
light shake of Worcester sauce
cranberry sauce or gravy to serve

Grease loaf tin about 17cm x 6cm x 6cm and heat oven 180°C / 160°C fan / gas 4.

Boil parsnip. Cube. Lightly oil frying pan and melt butter, sauté onion a few minutes before adding mushrooms and cook another 5 minutes. Give a final sauté with cooked cubed parsnip and chopped hazelnuts. Remove from heat. Place in a large bowl and combine with chestnuts, cheese, breadcrumbs and thyme. Season.

Finally bind everything together with a beaten egg. Spoon into tin and bake 45-50 minutes. Invert onto a warm plate. If serving with potatoes and vegetables, gravy might be preferred or if with a side salad, cranberry sauce.

Nut macaroni curry (serves two)

100-150g macaroni
6-8 florets of cauliflower, washed
1 tbsp curry powder
1 tbsp oil
1 tbsp flour
1 small onion
300ml vegetable stock
1 small pepper, finely chopped
50-75g cashew nuts

Cook macaroni as directed, popping in cauliflower to boil with it. Drain. Sauté onions and pepper in oil till soft. Add curry powder then flour to form a roux and cook 2 minutes. Gradually add stock on heat, stirring all the time. Simmer for 2 minutes till a smooth mixture. Stir in cauliflower and nuts. Serve with hot macaroni.

Variation: replace half stock with either milk or coconut flavoured milk, using ¼-inch coconut paste or a tbsp desiccated coconut.

Nutty sauce with pasta (serves two)

50g walnuts, pine nuts or cashews
pinch of thyme
salt and pepper
2-3 tbsp milk or cream

Blitz (liquidise all the above together.) When fairly smooth, gradually mix in the milk or cream. Add this to hot cooked pasta and mix well with fork so all pasta is coated. Serve sprinkled with fresh black pepper or chopped thyme.

Nutty Pilau (serves three-four)

Good with fried white fish fillets.

150g basmati rice (rinse till clear)
1 onion, finely chopped
30g butter
2 cardamom pods
1 garlic clove, pressed
pinch of turmeric or saffron optional
40g dried unsulphured apricots, chopped
300ml vegetable stock
50g pistachios (or pine nuts, almonds or cashews)
3 chopped cabbage leaves or handful of peas
optional: 40g raisins

Sauté onions in butter with a little salt till soft and golden. Add vegetables and sauté a minute or two. Crush cardamom and take time to smell the fragrance. Add cardamom seeds, garlic, and turmeric or saffron. Add rice. Pour stock over and bring to boil. Turn down heat, cover and cook 10-12 minutes or as packet directs till rice is tender. Stir in dried fruit if desired and nuts.

The Cuts of Meat

And their appropriate cooking methods

Lamb:

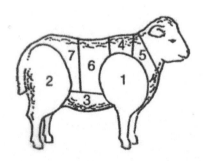

1	shoulder	roast / casserole
2	leg	roast
3	breast	roast / casserole
4	middle neck	casserole
5	scrag end	stew
6	best end	roast, grill, fry
7	saddle	roast, grill, fry

Beef:

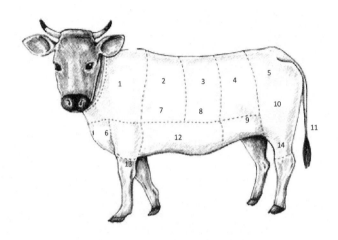

1	neck	casserole, stew, pot roast
2	chuck & blade	casserole, stew, pot roast
3	fore rib	roast, grill, fry
4	flank	roast, grill, fry
5	rump	roast, grill, fry
6	clod	casserole, stew, pot roast
7	feather	casserole, stew, pot roast
8	thin rib	roast, grill, fry
9	sirloin	roast, grill, fry
10	topside, silverside	roast, grill, fry
11	ox tail	casserole, stew, pot roast
12	brisket	casserole, stew, pot roast
13	shin	casserole, stew, pot roast
14	leg	casserole, stew, pot roast

Pork:

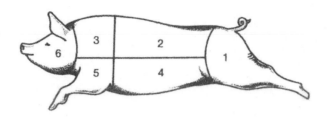

1	leg	roast, casserole
2	loin	roast, fry, grill
3	spare rib	roasting, pies
4	belly	roast, casserole
5	shoulder	roast, sausages, pies
6	cheek	casserole

Mighty meat dishes

SAVE the planet! Eat less meat, we are urged. If only that plea would cut sufficient mustard here. Our love of meat harks back to country squires who boasted of fattening their own geese to slaughter on their own land, to eat at Yuletide and have their pillows stuffed with the feathers. Is it this unconscious snobbery that draws Brits to choose meat for the main course?

A Yorkshire uncle once told us laughingly that in the war, if anyone in their road could afford a joint to roast on Sunday, a performance would be made of sharpening the carving knife at the window for the neighbours to see. Rather than prestige, perhaps meat is popular for its food value. I doubt it, despite its having the highest biological value protein, along with iron and vitamin B12, in a form most accessible to the body.

Eggs, cheese, fish, soya and nuts are nutritionally comparable yet we cling to meat, men especially. Marlon Brando in Williams' A Streetcar Named Desire arrives on set 'carrying a bloodstained packet of meat', immediately defining Stanley's macho character.

It would hardly be the same if he was carrying half a dozen eggs or a bag of nuts or even a packet of cheese. Anyway, when it comes to cooking meat, the part of the body from where the cut is made and the animal's age both inform the cooking.

Either the flesh is young and tender and may be dry cooked quickly by grilling or roasting or it is tougher and needs slow moist methods such as casseroling and stewing. A third possibility is in between which suits pot roasting or shallow frying with a later addition of moisture.

Olde English Roasts

Loin of pork or a fillet of beef are the easiest joints to roast and carve. Pork, served with homemade apple sauce and sage and onion stuffing, is my favourite. That said, I have been converted to roast lamb, having eaten the best of it at our local White Horse pub.

Chicken is the cheapest roast unless you buy free range which is both amazingly superior and much more expensive. The first time I roasted a free range chicken I realised that the fabulous aroma emanating from the oven was how roast chicken smelt in my childhood. It tasted better too. It is the same with apples and many other foods.

Modern foods lack flavour, probably because of destructive technological tricks perpetrated by today's processing methods. Perhaps this explains a certain dissatisfaction with food today and the craving for strong flavours. Look out for home reared, free range organic meat as it is likely to be superior in flavour. For classic gravy to accompany your roast see page 51.

Roast loin of pork

Oven 200°C / 180°C fan / gas 5. Moderate roasting for spare rib or loin 30 minutes per lb (450g), leg 35 minutes per lb (450g). To obtain crispy crackling rub salt and oil into scored skin before roasting. Stand joint on a rack to keep crackling out of dripping. Cook well, over rather than under. Remove joint and keep warm. Make gravy. See page 51.

Accompany with homemade English apple sauce made from glistening, pale golden, stewed, juicy Bramley apples (not out of a jar), roast potatoes and seasonal vegetables.

Roast chicken

Lay a free range chicken, giblets removed for gravy, on a roasting tray or dish and baste with some oil and a little butter. Roast in a moderately-hot oven 200°C / 180°C fan / gas 6 at 20 minutes per lb (450g) until breast is golden brown and skewer comes out clean, without a sign of blood, when inserted in the breast, or a meat thermometer reads 82°C.

(Optional: in the last 10-15 minutes spread a little paste made from a teaspoon each of soya sauce, crushed garlic and honey over the breast.)

Roast beef

Use tender joints like sirloin, fillet and ribs.
Roast at 220°C / 200°C fan / gas 7 for rare or
underdone allowing 15 mins per lb (450g) and 15
minutes over. (For medium to well done, oven
200°C / 180°C fan / gas 6 suits sirloin and rib.

Allow 25 minutes per lb. Boned and rolled and
thick pieces 30 minutes per lb.) Place meat in
roasting pan and sprinkle with flour and a little
salt and oil or dripping on top of meat. Baste
often. Lift out when a meat thermometer reads
71°C for medium cooked and make gravy in the
roasting pan. See page 51.

Yorkshire pudding

100g (4oz) plain flour
1 egg
300ml (½ pint) milk

Oven: 220°C / 200°C fan / gas 7. Sieve flour into bowl and make a
well in middle. Drop in 1 egg and ¼ pint milk. With a wooden
spoon beat egg and milk gradually drawing in flour. Beat well
(should sound like galloping horses) then slowly add another ¼
pint of milk and beat till smooth.

Either use a shallow tin about 15cm (6-inch) diameter or a bun tin
and pour in a little dripping from the joint. Heat oil in oven a few
minutes till very hot and almost smoking. Pour on batter and bake
for 15 minutes. Aim for a round crispy pudding with a golden
brown smooth wall and dropped centre. Not the multi-pointed
monstrosity often served in pubs.

Roast gammon (serves eight-ten)

Perfect for any family party even at Christmas, enjoy the roast and
carve on demand any left over for sandwiches. My daughter's lab-
rador approves too. Only having kept polite little dogs myself, I
forgot greedy Oscar could reach our kitchen units easily. On one

occasion, I came into the kitchen just in time to catch him sinking his teeth into the ham.

After my loud scream, he dropped it into my hands and I cut off the bit that bore his teeth marks, and a little more. It was not a pretty sight: his wild, wicked eyes shining with pleasure as he was about to demolish our Boxing Day dinner.

> **2.7kg (6-7lb) gammon joint**
> **4 tbsp port (for glazing)**
> **225g (8oz) plum jam**
> **300ml (½ pint) apple juice**
> **1 tbsp arrowroot if needed**
> **a lot of cloves**

Soak ham in water overnight. If bowl is too small to cover meat, turn over halfway or at some point but not 3 o'clock in the morning! Cooking time: Allow 20 minutes per lb (450g) plus 20 minutes over. Weigh joint and work out total cooking time.

I need a pencil and paper for this: Boil for half the cooking time (or pressure cook for a third of that half), eg 6lb x 20m = 2hrs + 20 minutes. So boil for 1 hour 10 minutes. (If using a pressure cooker follow its instructions which usually means divide by 3 ie pressure cook for 23 minutes.) Whilst it's boiling, heat oven to 180°C / 160°C fan / gas 4.

Then make glaze by simmering apple juice and jam for 5 minutes before adding port and simmering for another 5 minutes. Remove joint from water when ready and place in a foil lined roasting tin with a good edge of foil to wrap over sides if joint starts to over-brown anywhere.

Next, cut off rind and score fat into diamonds. Stud with cloves. Using a spoon or brush, glaze joint and roast meat for the other half of the cooking time: 1 hour 10 minutes. Baste often. Wrap edges of foil over areas of meat that darken. When cooked, allow joint to cool a little.

Carve and serve with a sauce boat of left over glaze which should be enough for eight. (If necessary, it may be thickened by blending two tbsp arrowroot (or cornflour) with a little water and adding to simmering glaze to bring to boil.) Gorgeous with good homemade mash and a selection of vegetables. Brilliant for entertaining as no last minute gravy making is needed and a meat thermometer reading of 70°c tells you meat is cooked.

Whilst I love the flavour of mustard and brown sugar or mustard and honey or just apricot jam, marmalade or cider and treacle, this glaze and sauce is the best!

Roast lamb

Welsh lamb in the spring and early summer is tender and tasty. The best joints for roasting are leg, shoulder and loin.

Allow 30 minutes per lb and use a moderately-hot oven at 200°C. The potatoes may be roasted alongside the meat and some chunks of onion for gravy. Remove and keep warm if cooked or browned earlier. Place joint in a roasting tin with oil for the potatoes. If a non-stick pan with handles is used it will be easy to lift it on the hob and make the gravy whilst the meat is being carved. See page 51.

Roast potatoes alongside joint if possible. They should be cut into even-sized pieces and may be par-boiled for 5 minutes first. Sprinkle lightly with salt. Bake for 30 minutes or more (or up to 60 minutes if not par-boiled) till golden, basting often with fat from roast. If cooking separate just brush with oil first. Turn over for even browning. Test with skewer for softness in the middle.

Hints for a perfect steak:

1. Find a butcher you trust.
2. Choose the cut. Rump is unreliable. Sirloin is better for both tenderness and flavour.
3. Look for marbling: steak with fine white / creamy veins. If in the mood, hit with a steak hammer.
4. Ensure steak has been at room temperature for 20 minutes. (It must be completely thawed if frozen.)
5. Dry steak between kitchen paper and heat a tbsp oil in frying pan.
6. When oil produces a blue haze (is almost smoking) sear the steak both sides then turn down heat to cook.
7. A thin steak cooks in a minute, a thicker one takes 3-4 minutes each side or more if plump, for well done.
8. Serve with thick sliced fried onion rings or horseradish sauce and mushrooms, salad, coleslaw and chips.

Find a butcher you can trust, like M.E. Evans, High Street, Overton-on-Dee

Photo by Ben Roberts

Round the World for quick, tasty minced beef dishes

Many countries have their traditional way of flavouring minced beef similar to the Bolognese method. In different parts of Italy, as in the culinary world at large, recipes vary. You can experiment. Traditional British minced beef dishes, given below, are beef cobbler and cottage pie. For maximum flavour, all these dishes improve with slightly slower cooking and standing the dish overnight gives maximum flavour.

Old Favourite Spaghetti Bolognese (serves three-four)

Bolognese sauce	**450g (1lb) minced beef, fried**
	100ml red wine
	1 or 2 tsp olive oil
	150ml beef stock
	1 big onion, chopped fine
	2 garlic cloves, chopped fine
	400g tomatoes
	1 tbsp tomato paste
	seasoning
	2 tsp dry oregano or thyme
optional:	**pinch of cinnamon**

Soften onions gently in hot oil before browning meat. Next add tomatoes, wine, stock, herbs and seasoning and simmer slowly for 20-60 minutes till thick. Allow 50g spaghetti or pasta per person. Cook as packet says. Place on plates with minced beef in the middle and a bowl of grated hard cheese to hand.

Mexican chilli con carne

This uses Bolognese sauce with added kidney beans (400g can) 1-2 tsp hot chilli spice in the mince. It makes a healthy dish when accompanied with rice (or cauliflower rice, see page 42) and salsa and guacamole or sliced avocado and plain yogurt or sour cream.

Moussaka

This is a casserole of a layer of mince cooked in a Bolognese sauce with a middle layer of sliced, cooked vegetables like courgette, aubergines or potato and another layer of mince. Top with Béchamel sauce or a mix of mascarpone with Greek yogurt and a sprinkling of grated cheese. Bake for up to 35 minutes at 200°C /

180°C fan / gas 6. If you want it to stand up for itself like a real Greek one, ensure the sauce and mince is not runny and leave overnight. Next day it should cut like a cake.

Spanish toreador pancakes

3 or 4 homemade pancakes or wraps
300ml (half a pint) cheese sauce
or 1/3 tub mascarpone
100g grated Cheddar cheese
450g (1lb) Bolognese sauce

Stuff each pancake with some Bolognese mince filling, roll up and place in oven-proof dish. Cover with mascarpone or cheese sauce and top with cheese and crumbs. (If using small tortillas, lay Bolognese mince on base of a dish, cover with a tortilla topped with mascarpone and repeat stacking.) Top with grated cheese. Bake 20 minutes, 200°C / 180°C fan / gas 6.

British beef cobbler

450g (1lb) Bolognese sauce
and in the cooking, add:
1 tbsp Worcester sauce
2 sliced cooked carrots

Topping is savoury scones: Place 200g SR flour in a bowl. Rub in 50g butter then add enough milk for a soft dough. Roll to an inch thick. Cut rounds. Place on cobbler and glaze with beaten egg or milk before baking 15-20 mins at 220°C / 200°C fan / gas 7.

South African bobotie (serves three-four)

450g (1lb) mince cooked with onion, beef stock and tomato paste (no tomatoes)

During cooking add:
Half a cup each of chopped apple, chopped dried apricots, sliced almonds.
Optional: a light sprinkling of sultanas and chopped ginger.

Soak two white bread slices in milk for 10 minutes or so. Press out excess liquid and put to one side. Make the mince base in the usual Bolognese way, adding the apple and 1 tbsp of curry powder whilst the mince is browning. Add apricots to meat as it simmers in beef stock. When cooked stir in soaked bread. Pour in casserole dish.

Make topping: Either moussaka topping as given above or make ½ pint white sauce and mix in a beaten egg.

Cool white sauce and add beaten egg and a little turmeric. Beat together. Pour over meat. Cover with flaked almonds. Bake for 180°C for about 25 minutes till topping is golden and set. (May be serve with boiled rice with ½ tsp turmeric.)

Italian lasagne

This is composed of layers of Bolognese sauce between pasta sheets and topped with cheese sauce. Bake according to instructions on lasagne packet, usually 35-40 mins at 200°C. Serve with a green salad and crusty bread.

American burgers

It is strange that a burger is more popular than a plain steak on a bap; the latter is tastier, quicker and healthier though more expensive. Perhaps we latched onto burgers as a nation for their American appeal as they crossed the pond about the same time as fast food joints like Wimpy. Cool, man.

400g minced beef
1 onion, finely chopped
1 round of breadcrumbs
salt and pepper optional
extra flavouring eg chilli
1 egg, beaten
(About 50g sausage meat may be added for a juicier burger.)

Mix all the ingredients together. Form into meatballs. (If time chill for 20 mins.) Press hard to flatten into burgers. Fry or grill about 5-6 minutes each side.

If in a hurry, ordinary, plain minced beef on its own works well enough when shaped into burgers but you can experiment with different extras like 1 tsp Worcester sauce or 1 tbsp tomato ketchup, a shake of garlic powder or ½ -1 cup of All Bran instead of breadcrumbs or all the lot together.

If the burgers are chilled prior to cooking they hold together especially well.

Favourite pork dishes

Pulled pork (serves eight)

1kg shoulder of pork, with bone and thick fat removed.

Place in slow cooker with barbecue sauce poured over and cook 5-6 hours.

Proper Barbecue sauce

To one chopped and fried onion, add:

1 cup BBQ sauce
¼ - ½ cup cider vinegar
½ cup chicken stock
¼ cup light brown sugar
1 tbsp English or American mustard
1 tbsp Worcester sauce
1 tbsp chilli powder
2 cloves garlic
½ tsp dried thyme

Po' boy

This is pulled pork and barbecue sauce served deliciously dripping into a French bread sandwich.

Mediaeval sausage and chestnut casserole (serves two-three)

A quick winter satisfier.

25g butter and 1 tbsp oil
1-2 onions, finely chopped
250g pork sausages (buy the best)
300ml beef stock
50ml strong wine such as Madeira,
port or ginger
1 dssp of blended cornflour or crème
fraiche
150g chestnuts (vacuum packed or
tinned)
fresh chopped parsley for garnish

Melt butter and oil, ideally in a casserole that is flame and oven proof. Fry chopped up sausages and onions till onion is soft and sausages browned. Add stock which has been flavoured with wine and well-seasoned. Bake for 20 minutes 200°C / 180°C fan / gas 6.

Thicken if needed with cornflour or crème fraiche. Garnish with parsley. Serve with mash and greens.

Porky chicken (serves four)

8 skinless, boneless, chicken thighs
8 rashers of smoked bacon
either 12oz (300g) pork sausage meat
or about 8 chipolatas, skinned
2 tsp chopped thyme

Preheat oven 200°C / 180°C fan /
gas 6. Mix sausage meat in bowl
with thyme. Shape into sausages that
fit into chicken thighs where the
bone was and fold meat around.
Wrap a rasher round each chicken
thigh, stretching it and hold together
with a cocktail stick. Place in oven
proof dish and roast for about 30-35
minutes. Serve with salad and your
favourite potatoes.

Bespoke sausages – made in seconds and delicious.

1kg minced pork
1 tsp fennel seeds
1 tsp chilli
100ml red wine
1-2 cloves garlic (or tsp of garlic salt)
salt and pepper

Mix all together by hand in a big bowl. Roll into a big sausage and keep dividing into two to make at least 12 sausages. If a softer texture is preferred stir in some cereal like finely milled oatmeal.

Bacon and barley hot pot (serves two)

Bacon is a good standby for a simple but substantial meal. This particular dish would also work well with a homemade boiled ham.

100g no-soak pearl barley
1 garlic clove, crushed
40g smoked back bacon
small handful prepared thyme
(or two tsp dried thyme)
½ onion, chopped
1 tsp smoked paprika
250ml chicken stock
1-2 tbsp tomato puree
100g button Brussel sprouts
shake of Worcester sauce

Follow instructions on barley packet which often means rinsing barley well, covering with cold water and bringing to boil. Instructions will indicate boiling and simmering time, at least 20-25 minutes. Drain.

Sauté onion and garlic in a frying pan for 2 minutes. Add bacon. Cook till onion is soft and golden. Add paprika, tomato puree and a shake of Worcester sauce then stock. Combine with barley and sprouts and season. Finally, either simmer for about 4-5 minutes till sprouts are cooked or casserole at 160-170°C for half an hour or so whilst you relax.

Special Party Dishes

Christmas casserole (serves six)

1-2 onions, chopped fine
175g bacon, chopped fine
brace pheasants, jointed
2tbsp oil, 2oz butter melted together
200g turkey breast
2 cloves of garlic
300ml port or sherry (or Madeira)
1 pint of chicken stock
sprig of thyme (washed)
1 bay leaf
175g each of cranberries and cooked
chestnuts, marinated in half the wine

Fry onions and bacon in flameproof casserole. Add joints and fry 5-6 minutes till golden. Add garlic and half the wine, stock, thyme and bay leaf and bring to boil. Cover and bake for at least 55-65 minutes at 170°C / 150°C fan / gas 3. Add redcurrant jelly and turkey breast and cook another 30 minutes till tender. Add cranberries and chestnuts and simmer 3 minutes. Taste and season before serving.

Moroccan lamb tagine (serves eight)

As a child, Morocco firmly implanted itself in my mind as romantic and exotic, probably from seeing too many films like Casablanca.

When my brother recently sent me an exciting description of his day visit there I was naturally jealous. I was enchanted by his words like medina, casbah, souk, bazaar and descriptions of labyrinthine streets with snake charmers and his experience of Moroccan food at a restaurant where a traditional band played.

When the chance came to do likewise, I seized it. Sadly, it seemed to me that the rushing inhabitants of the winding streets looked more like the cast of a Carry On or Monty Python film. I think it was the glimpse of the Levis and Nike trainers under the kaftans that spoilt the image.

And what is it about someone wearing a
fez that means you can't take them seri-
ously? Nevertheless, Moroccan food is fabulous but go gently with the spices when
you first make this sumptuous casserole. (A
later addition of cooked potatoes will tone
down the spice if you prefer it blander.)

1.1 kg (2½ lb) diced shoulder of lamb

Choose one of the following two methods to cook the diced lamb.
The second is quicker but may be a tad less tasty.

Either:

a) Marinade the lamb for 3 hours or overnight in fridge with:

2 tsp cumin mixed with ½ tsp or less of ground cloves
1 dssp ground coriander
seasoning
2 tsp dried thyme
4 crushed garlic cloves.
Add oil and orange juice and stir well.

Also marinade **apricots and raisins with sherry and vinegar** and
leave as above before proceeding with recipe.

Or:
*b) You can just get on with it as below and when cooked leave in
fridge overnight for flavours to mingle:*

150ml fresh orange juice
2 tbsp olive oil
100g (4oz) dried, chopped apricots
50g (2oz) raisins
200ml (6 fl oz) dry sherry
25ml (1 fl oz) vinegar (pref sherry)
3 tbsp plain flour
50g pine nuts
300ml (½ pint) lamb stock
½ tsp paprika

optional: **black olives, halved**

Heat a little oil in a large, flame-proof casserole and brown meat. Lower heat. Add flour to casserole and stir well. Add all liquid and stock to casserole. Stir well, bring to boil then season. Add spices and fruit and everything. Cover casserole with lid. Cook at 180°C / 160°C fan / gas 4 for about 1 hour 15 minutes or until meat is tender. Probably, an hour will do if you are heating it up later.

If desired, sprinkle with chopped parsley and some pine nuts or toasted almonds to serve. Boiled rice makes a good accompaniment. When cooking the rice, it is optional to add a sprinkling of saffron (expensive) or turmeric (inexpensive) to get a yellow colour and subtle taste.

This rich dinner party dish suits being made in advance for the best flavour. Variations include frying 1 or 2 chopped onions with the meat, adding tomato paste or tinned tomatoes or chickpeas or sliced courgettes. Other popular spices to flavour tagines are cayenne or paprika, bay leaf, nutmeg, ginger and cinnamon. Probably best to just try three at a time. Red wine may replace sherry. But I do like my recipe combination best.

A Chinese adventure

*St Thomas' school photo.
Stockton Heath, Warrington, 1957.*

'How would you like to go to a Chinese restaurant?' my big sister asked me one day. To a ten-year-old in the 1950s that was a dream. She met me at St Thomas' school, Stockton Heath, at 4 o'clock to get the bus to Manchester. Manchester! A restaurant! A Chinese restaurant! I would have my sister all to myself for ages.

I couldn't wait for the school bell to ring. We jumped on a red bus (they were all red then) and chatted as we crossed the Manchester Ship Canal and saw Cheshire fields turn to villages which turned into towns, till all was concrete, metal and hurtling traffic.

With an air of familiarity, she led me from daylight into the darkness of *The Lotus Blossom* with its dim red tasselled lanterns and crimson embossed wallpaper. Waiters, like huge blackbirds, darted about with menus, chopsticks and water. To be treated like a grown up is a wonderful thing to a child. Edna's mouth-watering choices were, 'Chow Mein with bean sprouts, water chestnuts and bamboo shoots, foo yung and Peking duck with young chow fried rice and sweet and sour prawns.'

First we tucked into crab soup and then little steaming gilded bowls began to arrive. I loved the concept of sweet and sour, and the different textures like crispy batter, soft rice and crunchy beansprouts. Our banquet ended with a glass of China tea. 'Heck, Edna,' I said looking at the floating weeds in the murky water, 'this looks like a sample of Ackers Pit.' 'Try it. It's good.' It was. The perfect finish. Time to leave.

It was many years before I again tried oriental food. In the Sixties, I fed some boyfriends on Vesta-produced packets of dried Asian dishes. Then I found this authentic Chinese recipe. It worked well and it was the first dish I cooked for my husband. I see now that it was just a stir fry. He loved it and no doubt expected a lifetime of culinary pleasure. I hope he hasn't been disappointed.

Sing Jen Chi Ting (serves four)

400g of 1-inch cubed meat from a 1.2kg (3lb) raw chicken
200g fresh bean sprouts
3-4 fresh slices of pineapple, cubed (tinned ok)
300ml (½ pint) of chicken stock
1-2 tbsp soy sauce
125g mushrooms, wiped and sliced
4tbsp flaked almonds (essential)
200g freshly-cooked boiled rice
1 tbsp oil

Wash rice under cold tap and then boil for required time. Meanwhile, heat oil in wok or frying pan and brown meat in oil. Add soya sauce. Add pineapple and mushrooms and sauté for 4 minutes then add beansprouts and heat through. Add stock and simmer for 10 minutes till all is cooked. Lightly toast almonds in a dry frying pan. Watch all the time as they soon burn. Serve the chicken stir fry on a bed of hot drained rice. Sprinkle with the lightly toasted brown almonds.

Boeuf Bourguignon (serves four)

This French classic is one of the simplest casseroles of all and a perfect balance of taste and texture. Made in advance, it suits entertaining and earns a place in anybody's repertoire.

> **650g stewing beef, cubed**
> **½ pint beef stock**
> **100g diced bacon**
> **½ pint red wine**
> **20g flour**
> **½ tsp each: nutmeg, thyme, sage**
> **salt and pepper**
> **1 clove garlic, pressed**
> **1-2 tbsp olive oil**
> **100g button mushrooms**
> **12 baby onions**

Coat meat in flour. Heat oil and sauté beef, onions and bacon till browned. Stir in left over flour. Slowly blend in stock then wine. Bring to boil and then simmer. Add rest of ingredients. Season to taste. Bake at 180°C / 160°C fan / gas 3 for about 2 hours till meat is tender. Either creamy mash, roast potatoes or twice or thrice cooked chips make a good accompaniment along with simply cooked seasonal vegetables.

Variations on this casserole are:

Greek stifado: omit bacon. Add a bay leaf and 1 tsp each of cinnamon and ground cloves.

Hotpot: meat, onions, sliced potatoes and carrots only.

Beef and ale stew: replace wine with ale and in the last 20 minutes dunk ½ oz dumplings in stew and simmer.

Carbonnade: towards end of baking, top with French bread slices pasted with Dijon mustard and brown at heat.

Coq au vin (serves four)

1-2 tbsp olive oil
½ tsp thyme and 1 bay leaf
4 chicken joints
salt and black pepper
100g bacon, chopped
2 tbsp tomato puree
12 baby onions
1 clove garlic, minced
100g button mushrooms
½ pint chicken stock
1 level tbsp rice flour
(or cornflour blended with
1 tbsp water)
½ pint red wine

Fry chicken in 1 tbsp olive oil then place in casserole. Sauté onions and garlic with bacon, adding more oil if needed till all is golden brown. Add to chicken. Blend puree with stock and red wine and pour over chicken. Add herbs, seasoning and mushrooms and cover.

Bake at 170°C / 150°C fan / gas 3 for up to an hour and stir halfway through. Test with a skewer for tenderness and cook an extra 20 minutes before testing again. To serve, thicken liquor – if necessary, rice flour may be scattered on and stirred. If using cornflour blend with water, add to liquor and, stirring all the time, bring to boil. Serve with a green vegetable and boiled or roast potatoes, or rice or even chips.

Bagging the Game – Well I'll be hanged

The hare was sitting upright in the morning sun as I looked down the barrel of George's shotgun. I knew then at ten years old, that I was no vegetarian. I could easily have pulled the trigger. But only if I was hungry, really hungry, like Edward in 'The Children of the New Forest.'

George often let me accompany him when hunting and fishing and from these trips came an enduring passion for nature. Forty years on I realised that to him, capture of the fish or game was all important. A jewelled kingfisher sitting on a nearby branch aroused only a passing interest as did the changing intricate patterns of the clouds above or the ripple of silver on the stream beneath.

To me, it was all wondrous and if you got a meal out of it, so much the better. A lot more fun than shopping in a supermarket. Game has the particular merit of being organic, nutritious, tasty and depending on your sources, cheap or free. If you have a slow cooker nothing need be a bother with meat.

Place it in the cooker with a glass of wine and some vegetables and check now and then. If you put a whole carrot in, a whole onion and some celery, you'll have enough liquor to make a good sauce or gravy. It can be that easy and the slow cooker can be left on low all day, a help to the full-time worker and family chef.

Hares

Hares are hung for about seven days. The hare season is August to March but it should not exist as hares are now endangered.

Hares are magnificent creatures. I love them like I love foxes: primeval, aloof, mysterious. Now I come to think about it, the similarities with my husband are astonishing. In about 2001, I was standing by a gate between two fields when a hare lolloped up and sat down beside me in broad daylight.

I hardly dared to breathe. Slowly I turned my head, running my eyes over its long beautiful ears, black in the inside in contrast to its golden body. The moment of our togetherness seemed ages then it casually lolloped off. Our dog appeared and gave chase but the hare effortlessly widened the gap disappearing over the horizon. Years earlier in the same field, I witnessed two March hares boxing. Our alert neighbours saw it first and gave us a ring. What a theatrical sight: the female fists going like the dong on an alarm clock. Apparently it is the Jill's second courtship test of the Jack's strength. The first test is running away over many miles to see if he can catch her. What a splendid idea.

I think all females should make the chase fun. If he catches her there is a good chance she will mate. If not, well he was not fit anyway. Having caught her, it is possible she is still not ready to mate. Then she will stand up and throw one punch or several. And nature's reason for this contrary behaviour? One theory is that hares live out in the open and speed is crucial for their survival. A hare can manage thirty-seven body lengths per second and cheetahs only twenty three. What a sight to witness. It saddens me to the core of my being that such sights are now rare.

We got our first and probably last hare courtesy of our dog, 'Whiskey' who was a small basenji cross. One summer evening this little timid dog chased a hare over a Cheshire field until the hare made the mistake of jumping into a ditch and the dog was on it instantly. A scream told us he had killed the hare.

I was both sad and practical. Hares were not rare then and I wanted to try jugging it. The result was one of the best meals ever with six or more hearty portions.

Here is the recipe in case a dead one falls into your lap or hopefully, hares become plentiful again.

Jugged hare (serves five-six)

1 hare, hung
25g butter
2 onions, chopped
2 sticks celery, chopped
2 carrots, sliced
900ml water
25g cornflour
1 tsp salt
a bouquet garni
1 wine glass of port
1 tbsp redcurrant jelly

Accompaniment of suet stuffing balls:

4oz white breadcrumbs
50g shredded suet
½ tsp salt
1 tsp mixed herbs
½ tsp finely grated lemon zest
milk to bind
oil and butter to shallow fry

Joint hare. Melt 25g butter in flame proof casserole and fry joints till brown. Remove. Add sliced vegetables to casserole and fry about 6 minutes. Replace hare in casserole and add water, salt and bouquet garni. Cover casserole and cook in centre at 180°C / 160°C fan / gas 4, for two to three hours till tender. Make stuffing balls by combining suet, seasoning, herbs and lemon zest and bind together with milk. Shape into 12 balls.

Fry gently in butter or oil till crisp and golden. Transfer cooked joints to a warm serving dish and keep hot. Mix flour to a smooth paste with a little water then add to casserole with redcurrant jelly. Bring to boil stirring well till it thickens. Add port and simmer 2 minutes. Remove from heat. Pour sauce over hare. Serve with stuffing balls, extra redcurrant jelly and game (very thin) chips.

Pan-fried partridge (serves two-three)

(Season runs September-January. Hang for about seven days.)

The partridge is small but the meat tender with a mild, interesting game flavour. Really very nice. There is often little fat on wild game so be careful not to overcook.

1 tbsp oil
small glass of red wine
2 sprigs thyme, de-stalked
4-6 partridge breasts
125-200ml chicken stock
4 slices black pudding
1 dssp of cranberry sauce

Heat oil and fry meat and black pudding up to 5 minutes each side. Remove. Keep warm. Deglaze pan with red wine. Stir well. Add stock, wine, thyme leaves and cranberry sauce and bring to the boil. Return meat to pan and heat through. Check for tenderness. Yes, it's that quick! Season. Serve with mash, roast potatoes or game chips, seasonal vegetables like carrots, button sprouts or braised red cabbage and some homemade apple sauce. This is a feast of flavours.

If you acquire a partridge, newly shot, take a moment to admire its beauty, particularly the more common French red legged variety before it is hung and skinned. I would not shoot anything myself without necessity or want to encourage others to shoot but I am not squeamish (any more) about eating dead animals.

Pheasant season, October – January

Pheasants should be hung for about seven days in a cold place to allow rigor mortis to wear off and lactic acid to develop which softens the fibres.

Plucking is easier while the bird is warm but skinning removes the feathers at the same time and is quicker. Having plucked or skinned, put your hand in the cavity and pull out the innards (giblets): an act of heroic bravery. (Simmer these for about 30 minutes, strain and add the liquor to make stock.)

Hopefully, someone will present you with a pre-hung, fleeced body resembling a little pink chicken. Some cooks throw the legs in the stock pot as they are spindly and difficult to eat. Given that pheasants are free range and shot, it is hard to ascertain age. Size apparently is no indicator but the 'nobble' on the beak grows and hardens with age.

Also old cock pheasants have pronounced back claws. Young tender birds may be roasted but mature tough birds need slow, moist cooking. If in doubt, stew, pot roast or slow cook.

Roast pheasant (serves two)

**1 young plumpish pheasant
15g butter
a small bunch of thyme, washed,
dried and chopped
salt and pepper
1-2 tbsp port or red wine
1-2 tbsp plain flour
1 tbsp oil
1 tbsp redcurrant or cranberry sauce
300ml stock**

Set oven to 190°C. Oil a roasting tin, add pheasant and dot with butter (wrap breast in bacon if liked). Sprinkle with salt and pepper and thyme and roast. Splash on a glass of wine if you're hedging your bets about its age. Roast for 35-45 minutes. To test if ready, pierce thigh with a skewer and juice should run clear.

A meat thermometer should reach 63°C in breast and 80°C in leg. Let bird rest in a warm place and make gravy by spooning off excess fat from roasting tin and gently heating the rest (about a tablespoon) on hob. Add enough flour to absorb fat (now a roux) and cook a minute or two before slowly stirring in red wine or port. Then add stock and bring to boil. While it is simmering, season and add a flat tablespoon of redcurrant jelly or even nicer, cranberry sauce.

Classic braised pheasant (serves four)

> **brace of birds, jointed into even pieces**
> **2 rashers back bacon**
> **2 tbsp oil**
> **1 stick of celery, washed and chopped**
> **1 tbsp flour**
> **150ml each of stock and wine**
> **2-3 sprigs thyme, washed & chopped**
> **2 tsp Worcester sauce**
> **1 tbsp redcurrant jelly**

Brown seasoned jointed pieces in hot oil in the frying pan. Fry bacon in the pan with celery, then pour stock over and add thyme. Add Worcester sauce and jelly and bring to boil before pouring over casserole. Place on lid. Casserole for at least 1½ hours at 160°C / 140°C fan / gas 3 (or the temperature your oven simmers the dish).

Slow-cooked pheasant

Ideal for tenderising meat, the slow cooker allows you time to get on with writing your novel or needle-point embroidery or worrying about when your speeding fine will arrive!

Oil the slow cooker lightly. Brown joints and onions in a frying pan. Place in slow cooker with 200ml stock and carrots and leeks. Cook for two to three hours. Test with a skewer for tenderness.

Slow-cooked guinea fowl (serves three-four)

The best compliment I ever received as a cook was when my daughter on her return from a foodie holiday in the south of France said the French food had been great but this dish was better!

1 large guinea fowl
glass of sherry (even better, Madeira)
8 chestnut mushrooms
1 small carton of double cream

Oil and heat slow cooker. Add guinea fowl. Add a glass of sherry and pour yourself one. Every half hour or so turn the bird round so that a different part is on the bottom of the cooker. It manages to go a pleasing golden brown in mine. Cook for about two hours. Keep warm. Keep the meat juices.

Make a sauce by frying chestnut mushrooms, adding fresh double cream, the meat juices and more Madeira or sherry. (Not for you.) Finally, the bird looks like it has been roasted and combines gorgeously with the sherry sauce.

Rabbit in mustard sauce (serves four well)

Rabbit should be hung 4-5 days. It is available all year but best September to February. Farmed rabbit is bigger than wild usually.

1 large rabbit, hung and jointed
4 tbsp butter
½ cup double cream
2 chopped onions (large)
1 tsp dried thyme
½ cup French mustard
4 tbsp chopped parsley
½ cup white wine
½ cup water
600ml (1 pint) of stock
optional extra: 4 slices back bacon, chopped

Using a frying pan, brown rabbit joints in butter. Remove pieces. Add bacon if using and onions and brown for 3-4 minutes. Add wine, mustard and water. Bring to boil. Season. Place rabbit in casserole and simmer from 45 minutes to an hour on hob (or in oven at 170°C / 150°C fan / gas 3-4 for 1-2 hours) or till meat is nearly falling from the bone. Remove cooked rabbit to a warm place. Reduce sauce by vigorous boiling and stirring till half of it is left. Add cream, parsley and rabbit. Heat through and serve.

Wild duck in blackberry (or blackcurrant) sauce (serves four)

Hang 2-3 days. Season: September to January.

Of all the species of wild duck, mallard is the biggest and usually feeds two whereas teal and widgeon are small necessitating one bird each. Take care not to overcook wild duck as the meat is leaner and less fatty than a domestic duck. The blackcurrant sauce is quicker. Both are delicious.

230g (10oz) blackberries
sprig of thyme, washed & de-stalked
1 tbsp sugar
small wine glass (100ml) ruby port
small wine glass (100ml) red wine
two mallards: hung, plucked, jointed
100ml orange juice
stock
blackberry (or blackcurrant) juice
Continued overleaf:

	10g butter and 1 tbsp olive oil
	salt and pepper
	100g (4oz) mushrooms, sliced
	1 tbsp cranberry sauce
	1 red onion, sliced
optional:	1 or 2 star anise

Reserve three berries each for garnish. Make syrup (possibly the day before) by placing berries in a small pan, sprinkling with sugar and enough water to cover and gently simmer a few minutes till soft. Blend or bash till smooth and finely sieve to remove seeds.

Now for the main part. Fry joints in oil and butter on both sides till golden brown, at least 3 minutes each side. Legs take longer so start cooking them first. Remove meat. Sauté onion 2 minutes. Add mushrooms and sauté 2 minutes. Slowly add wine, stock, blackberry (or blackcurrant) syrup, star anise if using and return the nearly cooked duck meat. Bring to boil and heat through a few minutes for rare or longer for well done. Poke with a knife to see if tender. Stir in cranberry sauce. Serve with a seasonal vegetable, mashed potato (or mashed celeriac or broad beans) or chips or roasties.

If you buy a domestic duck, roasting is an easy way to cook it. Lightly rub salt onto skin and prick skin with skewer to let the fat out. Place on a rack in a roasting tin in a very hot oven at 200°C / 180°C fan / gas 6 for 15 minutes then lower to 180°C / 160°C fan / gas 4 for about 1½ hours. Or 15 mins per lb + 15 mins. Basting should not be necessary but draining fat occasionally is. Any sauce brushed over bird towards the end should give an attractive glaze.

Frattaglie (Offal)

"What fat cheeks you ha' got.
Darn me if I couldn't eat them . . . get me a file or
I'll have your heart and liver out."

Charles Dickens' Great Expectations

(Hmm, which goes best with a nice glass of chilled Chianti: cheeks, heart or liver? I'd go for the cheeks. If you find yourself in this cannibal situation, here are the best recipes for serving the best parts of frattaglie or offal, as it is less elegantly known.)

Cheek goulash (serves four) – absolutely divine

1kg ox cheeks (2), each cut in two
2 onions, sliced thinly
3 garlic cloves, crushed
2 tbsp oil
1 tbsp flour
1 tsp smoked paprika
1 tbsp sweet paprika
300ml ale
500ml beef stock
2 bay leaves (or a bouquet garni)
2 tbsp fresh thyme
1 tbsp tomato puree
optional: **1 stick celery, sliced finely**

Fry seasoned cheeks in flameproof casserole till golden brown all over. Remove. Add onions and sauté for about 5 minutes till soft. Add garlic and fry for a minute. Then stir in flour and cook a minute or two. Add paprika, celery and ale and slowly bring to boil. Add stock.

Add bay leaves and return cheek. Cover with lid and simmer on hob's lowest setting for about 3½ hours till meat is cooked through and tender. Stir regularly and carefully as meat may break up. (It may also be baked in the oven at about 160°C / 145°C fan / gas 3-

4, just simmering.) Check if it is cooked (soft) after 2½ - 3 hours. Garnish with chives and serve with boiled rice or roast or mash potatoes and seasonal vegetables.

Pig's cheek is delicious too and appears more often on pub menus these days. If cooking for two, halve the above recipe and use 125ml sherry instead of ale and 275ml stock. Add ½ tsp cumin. Casserole in oven for 1½-2 hours at 160°C / 145°C fan / gas 3-4.

In Victorian England, offal was a staple food of the industrial poor as it was cheap; fortunately for them it is also highly nutritious. The flavour and texture vary according to the age and type of animal.

Calf's liver is considered the best and lamb's a close second. It is more expensive today because of a decline in popularity except in the best London restaurants where it now enjoys a revival. It is also still popular in Europe, of course, where they maintain their culinary traditions.

Liver and onions (serves two)

This dish makes the simplest, easiest and best gravy ever.

	2 pieces of lamb's liver
	(or the slightly stronger pig's liver)
	1 onion, finely chopped
	flour for coating
	oil for frying
	300ml (½ pint) beef stock
optional:	**2 rashers bacon, finely chopped**

Gently fry onion (and bacon if using) 5 minutes in hot oil till soft and translucent. Lightly flour liver and brown both sides. Add a little red wine (if desired) and stock. Slowly bring to boil, stirring.

Cook for up to 20 minutes for well-cooked and serve with freshly chopped parsley garnish and creamed or chipped potatoes, carrots or any seasonal vegetable available.

Stuffed lambs' hearts (serves four)

Hearts are delicious and nutritious and not over demanding to cook. If the hearts have not been properly prepared you will need some sharp surgical style scissors to trim away any odd bit of arteries and fat. Trim through the heart chambers too to make a good cavity for stuffing. Wash and dry.

4 lambs' hearts
4 slices back bacon

Stuffing:

1 small onion, chopped
30g butter
50g washed, sliced mushrooms
75g sausage meat
salt & pepper
1 tsp each dried parsley and tarragon

Sauce ingredients to pour over the stuffed, bacon-wrapped hearts:

1 tbsp of oil
1 tbsp plain flour
glass red wine
200g tinned tomatoes
200ml beef stock
splash of Tabasco or Worcester sauce

Oven 175°C / 150°C fan / gas 4. Make stuffing: sauté onion in butter. Add mushrooms and fry a few minutes before combining with sausage meat, seasoning and herbs. Stuff prepared hearts. Wrap in bacon, secure with a cocktail stick. Heat oil in frying pan and brown all over. Transfer to casserole.

Make sauce by simmering tomatoes. wine, stock, Tabasco and seasoning for 2-3 minutes. Pour over hearts. Bake for 1½ - 2 hours at about 170°C in a lidded casserole, basting occasionally till as tender as your heart. Serve with steak knives so that it can be sliced thinly as you eat it dipped in the rich gravy and mashed potatoes.

Just Desserts

WHY compete with nature? In Italy, it is the practice to place a bowl of fresh fruit on the table for dessert, so I was told by an Italian hairdresser. I believed her. She had an 18-inch waist. In Greece, a small plate of fresh cherries, grapes or melon is often served 'gratis' after your main course and very welcome it is.

Here are some interesting ways to make fresh fruit the centre of desserts and satisfying a little of that sweet craving.

Baked or fried bananas

This recipe also works well with fresh apples, pears, peaches and pineapple. Allow one banana per person at least. If cooking a lot, baking in a shallow casserole in the oven is easier.

Peel bananas and slice lengthwise, sprinkle with brown sugar and rum for adults. Melt a slither of butter and fry both sides till golden. If using harder fruit, slice thinner and cook longer. Serve with cream or ice cream.

Butterscotch bananas may be made as above but with syrup instead of sugar or a mixture of both. After frying till golden, add cream and stir well. Heat through for a few minutes. Serve.

Banana mint ice cream (serves four)

This is a last-minute, hands-on effort and therefore not suitable for large numbers. Most edible berries can replace the peas.

	4 frozen sliced bananas
	sprig of fresh mint
	250g (9oz) frozen peas
	2 tbsp agave syrup
optional:	**half a lime or lemon**

Blitz all ingredients. Serve at once.

Summer fresh fruit salad

First make a syrup by dissolving about 100g sugar in ½ pint of near boiling water. Prepare the fruit by peeling and adding this and any other unwanted bits to the cooling syrup to steep a while.

When it is cold, a little Grand Marnier or Cointreau may be added. Delectable. Cut fruit into chunks. Strain cold syrup over and chill.

This is a good dish for entertaining and making in advance, especially with liquor. For every day, prepare fruit just before the meal and omit the syrup or sugar if the fruit is sweet enough. If it is not, a drizzle of honey or maple syrup may be added. Use fruit in season.

Warm winter fresh fruit salad

As well as a dessert, this makes a very satisfying start to breakfast on a cold winter's day especially when figs and sultanas may be added. Figs and all dried fruit are especially high in calcium. On a  cold summer's day fruit may be varied to suit the season with perhaps some combination of strawberries, peaches and warm stewed rhubarb.

> **2 sliced bananas**
> **2 apples, peeled and sliced**
> **some apple juice**
> **2 oranges**
> **½ tsp ginger**
> **4oz (100g) grapes**
> **½ tsp ground cinnamon**
> **1 tbsp honey**
> **½ tsp grated nutmeg**
> **a little butter**
> **optional:** **chopped figs and sultanas**

Melt butter slowly, add fruit, honey and spices and caress in the hot fat a few minutes and serve warm.

Greek style orange salad
___

This was how it was served at Nico's, Kalami, Corfu: spoon yogurt onto the base of a plate. To remove the peel and pith from the orange, use a sharp knife in a circular, sawing downward motion starting at the top of the fruit and saw a continuous inch wide strip (over the serving plate to collect the inevitable escape of juice.) Next slice the orange horizontally and arrange over yogurt. Crumble walnuts on and dribble honey over. Simple but yummy.

Fresh fruit jelly
___

Simple and fun to make, home-made jelly tastes more tangy and refreshing than bought packet jelly. Read the directions on the gelatine packet. Mine says a pint (570ml) of jelly requires 12g of gelatine powder to set it. I use a measuring jug and water to top it up to a pint to achieve a perfect wobbly texture.

**2 oranges
1 lemon
1 sachet of 12g gelatine
70g sugar**

In a small bowl add ½ cup of cold water and sprinkle gelatine over. Stand this bowl in a shallow pan of water over a low heat and leave till it dissolves and goes transparent. (The gelatine must not boil.) Whilst it is dissolving, add sugar to a small pan of about 200ml of water and heat till it dissolves.

Peel the rind off with a vegetable peeler to include no bitter pith. Add rind to syrup and allow it to infuse for 15 minutes. Squeeze juice from fruit and put to one side. The syrup must not boil. Cool. Strain syrup into a 2 pint jug and add fruit juice and dissolved gelatine and enough water to make a pint (570ml) liquid. Stir gently. Pour into moulds and set in fridge.

Summer raspberry and elderflower jelly (serves four portions)
___

June is the best time to serve this when the flower and fruit are in season. It looks very elegant in big wine glasses. Decorate with culinary bought rose petals.

Check instructions on the gelatine packet. Mine say 4 gelatine leaves sets a pint of liquid. Leaf gelatine is more expensive but gives a clearer finish to the jelly.

2½ gelatine leaves
8-10 fl oz (½ pint) sparkling wine
2½ fl oz elderflower cordial
50g caster sugar (or xylitol)
a few raspberries, rinsed

Soak gelatine leaves in cold water in a shallow bowl up to 10 minutes till softened. Squeeze out excess water. Over a low heat dissolve sugar in cordial. Add softened gelatine leaves to syrup. Do not boil but melt gelatine slowly over a low heat. Cool. Stir in wine. Pour into glasses.

Add raspberries. Chill three hours. When set the jelly may be decorated with a little fruit or rose petals. (Culinary petals are sold at big supermarkets. If using your own petals, check they have not been sprayed. Wash well and pat dry.)

Mulled wine jelly, quick and tasty (an adults-only treat)

As the mulled wine already has spices all that is needed is:

60g caster sugar
300ml (½ pint) water
12-15g powered gelatine
300ml (½ pint) mulled wine

Dissolve gelatine by sprinkling onto a half cup of cold water which is placed in a shallow pan of hot water and kept hot till gelatine is transparent. Meanwhile make syrup by adding water and sugar to a saucepan and slowly bring to the boil and stir till sugar is dissolved. Cool. Pour mulled wine into a measuring jug. Add dissolved transparent gelatine and cooled syrup and gently stir to-gether. Pour into dish(es) and set in fridge. Decorate with fresh fruit and serve with cream.

Poached pears

(Also an attractive dish for the Christmas table)

Per person: 1 ripe conference pear, peeled
                         small lump of butter
                         1 glass of red wine
                         1-2 tsp caster sugar
                         ¼ pint water, more if needed

If you are in a hurry, cut the pears in half lengthwise (carefully try to remove core) and place in pan, sprinkle with sugar and sauté in a knob of butter both sides for a minute. Add wine and simmer for up to 15-20 minutes till soft when tested with a skewer. Serve with the wine syrup which can be boiled (remove pears first) to reduce and thicken it if necessary.

For special occasions leave pears whole with stem on. Thinly slice base so pear stands up. Simmer in wine till red all over, about 40 minutes. Again, lift out pears when soft and reduce wine by boil-ing fast till it becomes a syrup to accompany.

Gooseberry and elderflower fool (serves two)

Elderflowers blossom in early June when gooseberries ripen.

                         250g gooseberries, topped and tailed
                         2 tbsp caster sugar
                         6 medium elderflower heads, rinsed
                         150ml double cream, whisked
optional: 1 tsp elderflower cordial

Place fruit and flowers in a pan with lemon zest. Barely cover fruit with water and add sugar. Simmer for about 15 minutes till soft. Cool. When cold, whip cream until it leaves a trail. Once the gloss has gone, stop immediately or butter will be made which cannot be reversed. Fold whisked cream into stewed fruit and flowers. Chill for two hours. Serve each dish with a sprig of elderflower.

Autumn baked apples

Easy, delicious and a good use of oven space when cooking something else like a roast or casserole. The stuffing is usually either mincemeat or a mix of brown sugar (or honey), with dried fruit and butter. Optional flavourings are a pinch of cinnamon or ground nutmeg.

Oven 180°C / 160°C fan / gas 4. Prepare stuffing as suggested above. Core baking apples. Cut a piece from the core to make a plug for the bottom of each apple. Place apples in an ovenproof dish that has some water on the bottom. Spoon stuffing in. Either microwave for 4 minutes each or bake 35-40 minutes for dessert apples and up to an hour for Bramley baking apples, basting with juice a couple of times.

Mango brûlée

The dish gets very hot so handle carefully.

1 large ripe mango, sliced
1 tsp cinnamon
thick Greek yogurt
brown sugar

Place mango on bottom of heat-proof dish. Sprinkle over cinnamon and brown sugar and spoon over the yogurt until it covers it. Heat grill high. Place dish under for 3-5 minutes till golden brown.

Berry brûlée

Place washed berries in ovenproof dish. Fold equal amounts of lightly whipped cream into fresh Greek yogurt (with a sprinkle of sieved icing sugar if desired and a drop of vanilla essence). Cover with soft brown sugar and grill about 3-5 minutes till golden brown and bubbling. Careful as it soon burns and smokes! I prefer the next, safer recipe.

No-grill crème brûlée

In a shallow dish, place fruit such as sliced fresh peaches (though fruit is not necessary to this dish). Cover with a thick layer of yogurt. Sprinkle on dark Demerara sugar and leave in fridge for a couple of hours or more before serving. No grilling! No firemen! But it's quick to prepare and delicious to eat.

Poached peaches in berry sauce

Place in jug one fresh perfect peach per person. Pour over boiling water. Stand a few minutes till peach peels easily. Cut in half to remove stone. Stand peach halves in a serving dish. Make sauce by blitzing per person a dessertspoon of sugar with 50g strawberries, raspberries or blackberries or all three! Serve with cream.

Smoothies make delicious sauces for poached fruit desserts or ice cream. You can make as much as you like, when you like with whatever ingredients you like and thus avoid having to use up bought products that end up at the back of the fridge growing a fur coat.

Quince egg custard (serves two-three)

1lb quinces, peeled, cored, chopped
¼ cup sugar
1 tsp lemon juice

Peel and chop quinces into small chunks. Cover lightly with sugar, water and a tsp lemon juice. Bring to the boil and simmer 45 minutes - 1 hour till soft. Top up with more water if needed.

Make a baked egg custard mix and pour into a shallow casserole: see page 128 (or for a richer custard add an egg yolk, ¼ pint double cream and 2 tbsp each of ground almonds and golden caster sugar). When custard is baked, top with the stewed quince. (Some flaked almonds may go on the top. Serve hot or cold with cream.)

This is a simple yet delicious dessert. The quinces fill the room with a wonderful aroma and have an unusual but lovely flavour.

The Pie and Pudding Club

SWEET tarts are irresistibly delicious but the pastry base may be a health challenge. However, pastry can be replaced by a tasty nut or homemade biscuit base mixture which is healthier and quicker to make. Often baking is not needed and the crunchy texture works especially well with cheesecakes.

Nut or biscuit bases as alternatives to pastry tarts

For an 8-inch round tin try any of the following alternatives to pastry:

i. 200g crushed nuts mixed with 100g melted butter
ii. 300g crushed pecans or almonds mixed with ½ tsp salt and 220g medjool dates all blitzed together
iii. 200g plain homemade biscuits crushed and mixed with 100g melted butter
iv. 100g pecan nuts, 175g hazelnuts, both crushed and mixed with 100g melted butter
v. 100g crushed nuts and 50g crushed rough oatcakes, both mixed with a small egg
vi. 35g melted dark chocolate. Mix 50g crushed nuts with 40g crushed oatcakes. Beat in half a beaten egg and then the melted chocolate.

Some recipes for nut bases include brown sugar but I think it tastes too sweet and gritty. However for a chocolate filling a good pinch of spice like cinnamon or ground mixed spice or both, works well.

Line the cake tin and press the base mixture down before setting in the fridge.

Lemon cheesecake

Use any combination of yogurt or cream cheese (such as mascarpone) if you don't have quark.

**350g quark
(or low fat soft white cheese)
3-4 tbsp sugar
(or xylitol sugar substitute)
150ml (5 fl oz) double cream
a lemon, finely grated then juiced**

Add to the cream cheese lemon rind and juice, whipped double cream or yogurt and as little sugar as you can bear to suit your taste. (Yogurt may also be used alone as a 'mock' filling if it is placed on top and the whole pie is frozen.)

Whisk it all together till thick and spoon this mixture on top of the base and chill. Decorate if desired with sliced green grapes or other fruits or nuts or finely grated lemon rind.

Almond-based tarts

**55g (2oz) softened butter
50g (2oz) caster sugar
55g (2oz) ground almonds**

Glaze: gently melt 300g (10oz) redcurrant jelly with a tbsp water or lemon juice for a minute or two till dissolved.

Heat oven to 190°C / 170°C fan / gas 5. Cream the butter till soft then work in sugar and almonds. Spoon into 18cm (7-inch) diameter tins. Flatten out with spoon or hand. Bake for 20 minutes till golden brown.

Cool a little till not too soft to turn out. Fill with fresh forest fruits like strawberries, raspberries and blueberries or pureed fruit. Glaze with warmed redcurrant jelly.

Croustades

These little bread tarts are quick and a good way for children to learn rolling out skills before progressing to pastry.

3 slices of bread, white or brown
40g (1½ oz) butter

Oven:180°C. Roll the bread to make it thin. Stamp out rounds with pastry cutter to suit size of bun tin. Melt butter and brush tin. Press rounds in and brush inside of cases with melted butter. Bake 15-20 minutes till golden brown. Sweet cases may be filled with mincemeat or stewed apple. Savoury cases might use garlic butter and be filled with liver pâté or cream cheese and salmon. Good for buffet parties. If you just need 1 or 2 tarts, lightly fry both sides instead of baking. Shape into a tart whilst warm, not hot.

Pumpkin pie

When I taught Home Economics my A-level class was a joy. They chose their own dishes, first passed by me, to suit different assignments. Often, all I had to do in the practical class was oversee it, make encouraging remarks and sample the excellent results. The theory class was a different matter. It embraced chemistry, sociology and physics and I still get nightmares about it. My star pupil gave me this recipe. He became a Head Chef in a hotel in the Lake District I believe.

300ml (½ pint) cooked pumpkin
3 eggs
¼ tsp ground ginger
2 tbsp brandy
¼ tsp nutmeg
150ml (¼ pint) milk
good pinch of cinnamon
100g caster sugar

Heat oven 190°C / 160°C fan / gas 4. Line a 9-inch flan dish with 200g short pastry. Stir spices into stewed, sieved pumpkin. Next beat in eggs, brandy and enough milk to give a thick batter-like consistency. Sweeten to taste. Turn into pastry-lined flan dish. Bake for about 40-45 minutes.

Spicy sweet potato pudding

200g cooked sweet potato
1 egg
dash of cinnamon
57ml evaporated milk
dash of mixed spice
50g agave or maple syrup

Line a 9-inch flan tin with a healthier option base as above. Bake pierced sweet potatoes in their skins in microwave for 2 or 3 minutes, cool and scoop out flesh. In a bowl mix cooked potato with a teaspoon of cinnamon and mixed spice, a beaten egg, 57ml evaporated milk and 50g of maple or agave syrup. (Former is nicer.)

Bake at 180°C / 160°C fan / gas 4 for about 30 minutes till firm-ish. Test by putting the sharp edge of a small knife in the middle. Serve with yogurt whisked with cream and a dash of cinnamon.

Mock egg custard

Two boiled and finely mashed parsnips mixed with:
1 beaten egg
1 tbsp milk

Bake in a pastry-lined bun tin for 20 minutes at 200°C. It tastes very like an egg custard. It is a quick, tasty old Elizabethan recipe.

Proper baked egg custard (serves two-three)

Beat together 1 egg, 1tbsp sugar and 300ml (½ pint) of warm milk. Flavour with 2 drops vanilla essence or a little freshly grated nut-meg. Pour into half pint pie dish.

Bake 170°C, fan 150°C, gas 3, 40-45 mins. Test for set in middle by making a slit with a sharp knife.

Mediaeval lemon syllabub (serves three-four)

I like ancient recipes that link us to the past. This one is utterly de-lectable and so simple to make. It can be titivated with berries and a sprig of mint or rose petals.

1 150ml tub of double cream
1 small lemon, grated and juiced
1 dssp caster sugar
1 tbsp sherry or white wine

Whisk the cream till it's thick but not quite making peaks. Add the other ingredients and whisk till it peaks. Always take care with cream not to over whisk. As soon as the cream loses its gloss turn off the electric whisk and continue by hand if necessary as over-whisked cream turns to butter. This process cannot be reversed. Taste if it's sweet enough. Serve chilled.

Lemon posset (serves six-eight)

I called this posset as a reminder of its evolution from junket through to trifle, fool or syllabub. Whatever you call it, its tangy taste is simply delicious and it is easy to make. It suits being served in small, individual ramekin dishes or earthenware pots. These may be frozen if you make more than you need.

350g (14oz) tin condensed milk
4 lemons
250g (10oz) tub whipping cream
a few halved grapes for decoration

Finely grate lemons. Cut in half and press for juice. Whisk condensed milk till it becomes paler and/or a little thicker. Separately, whisk cream but not enough to lose gloss. Add condensed milk and whisk together. Mix in lemon rind and juice. Chill.

Cranachan

30ml (10 fl oz) fresh double cream
2-3 tbsp honey
2 tbsp whisky
50g toasted oatmeal
350g (2oz) raspberries

Lightly toast oatmeal in frying pan. Cool. Whip cream till nearly thick then whisk in honey and whisky till soft peaks form. Fold in fruit and oatmeal, reserving a little for topping. Spoon into glass dish (es).

Chocolate avocado mousse (serves three)

4 ripe avocados (ripe ones give slightly when pressed)
1 rounded tbsp coconut oil
dollop of maple syrup (optional extra sugar)
1 cup raw cacao powder (cocoa will do)
optional: 1 tsp balsamic vinegar

Mash the avocados till smooth. Mash in all the ingredients except cacao till smooth. Add cacao to taste till it looks chocolatey. Serve topped with fresh raspberries and/or chopped hazelnuts. (It freezes well.)

Another version consists of 3 avocados, ¾ cup almond milk, heaped cacao or cocoa and ¼ cup maple syrup or agave nectar. Cocoa is cheaper than cacao and not quite as pure.

Mississippi mud pie (serves four)

Appropriate to its origins in the Deep South, in making this pie you must 'cool' and 'chill' a lot.

175g double cream (or Greek yogurt)
37g crushed rough oatcakes
100g (70% cocoa) dark chocolate
2 eggs
50g crushed nuts
1 tsp vanilla essence
1 tbsp agave syrup
optional: **1 tsp each of cinnamon, mixed spice**

Heat oven 180°C and line 15cm (6-inch) cake tin. Place into a bowl 37g (half) chocolate broken up and melt over a pan of simmering water. Cool. Mix crushed nuts, oatcakes and half the melted chocolate then add half a beaten egg. Spoon this into non-stick or lined 20cm shallow cake tin and chill for 10 minutes. Melt remaining chocolate, keeping a piece to grate on top. Cool.

Mix 125g cream or yogurt with the remaining 1½ beaten eggs. Add vanilla, agave syrup and spices. Finally, beat in melted chocolate. Spoon into tin. Place on a baking tray and bake 20-25 minutes till set but wobbly. Cool. Chill 2 hours. Whisk cream till it peaks and dollop on (or use the remaining yogurt) and top with grated chocolate and optional pecans.

Butterscotch apple crumble (serves four)

With thanks to Carol at Shropshire's Derwen College who invented this when she had some butterscotch sauce to use up. It is delicious.

In a casserole place 400-450g Bramley stewed apples covered with butterscotch sauce made by melting 25g butter with 25g syrup, 25g dark brown sugar and 75g double cream. Top with crumble. Bake at 190°C for about 25-30 minutes.

Sweet Skirlie crumble, see page 49, is ten times tastier than the average crumble and no extras are needed.

Rice puddings

Rice puddings are in fashion again and drooled over by TV 'foodies' as the ultimate comfort food. I cannot disagree. Filling and cheap, milk puddings are especially nutritious for growing children. They can be made with any rice such as Indian, Thai or Italian and simmered on the hob or baked in the oven.

The hob is quicker but requires your full attention. The oven baked pudding requires little attention and makes economical use of oven space when another dish is being baked.

My Mum's brown skin rice pudding (serves two-three)

I told a lie when I said my mother only made pea soup and hotpot. She also made an excellent rice pudding. George and I fought over the caramelised brown skin after I had overcome my aversion to the word 'skin'.

> **600ml (1 pint) milk (full fat)**
> **50g rice, preferably pudding rice**
> **25g granulated sugar**

Wash rice under the tap before placing in an oven-proof container with sugar and milk. (For a richer pudding, add a little knob of butter.) Bake in a moderate oven, 180°C / 160°C fan / gas 4 for at least an hour to get the crispy brown top. Or it can be baked for 2 hours or longer on a lower heat.

Thai coconut and mango rice pudding (serves two-three)

Apparently, this is a Thai children's breakfast dish. It is flavoured with coconut and mango. Thai sticky rice may need soaking for 15 minutes first. (See packet.) This will soften it so you might need less milk.

> **600ml milk**
> **a fresh mango**
> **25g granulated sugar**
> **2 tbsp desiccated coconut**
> **or 25mm (an inch) of coconut cream**
> **50g Thai rice, rinsed**

Simmer milk, sugar, coconut and rice for about 15-20 minutes, stirring occasionally until the rice is tender and a pudding consistency is achieved. Pour in bowls and top with sliced fresh mango. Mmmh! Mango and coconut go together well.

Moroccan rice pudding (serves three-four)

This is made on the hob as above. It has the lovely touch of a rose syrup and rose petal topping. Pesticide free petals of high culinary quality can be found in most supermarkets.

> **75g Arborio rice**
> **25g caster sugar**
> **1 pint milk**
> **1 tbsp culinary rose water**
> **optional:** **rose syrup for drizzling**
> **rose petals for decorating**

Cook as in Thai recipe above but a little more slowly for up to 30 minutes. Stir often especially towards the end. It is firmer than most rice puddings but may be softened at the end with more milk. Either serve warm or chilled. Scatter on petals and a drizzle of rose syrup. Chopped pistachio nuts are an optional decorative touch.

Indian rice pudding (Kheer) is cooked during Indian religious festivals known as 'Pujas' which accompany 'Holi', the Hindu festival of colours, I believe.

Simmer for a good half hour in the proportion of 50g rice, 25g sugar and 600ml milk. Flavourings include either cardamom, cinnamon, almonds, cashews or pistachios or nutmeg, butter and a good tablespoon of dried fruit but not all at once! Perhaps two or three of your choice.

Scandinavian rice pudding

A traditional Christmas dish served hot or cold.

Add finely chopped, blanched almonds to finished rice pudding and one whole almond which merits a prize for the lucky recipient. A little cream is an optional extra or cherry compote, made by lightly stewing pitted cherries with sugar, thickening with cornflour or arrowroot and optionally flavouring with kirsch.

Greek halva (serves 2-3 but double for a hungry family of four)

When I was trying to buy this in Greek shops, I was often shown halva nougat by mistake. I would explain that I was looking for the halva pudding and then a soft, sentimental smile of nostalgia would pass over the Greek face as they remembered eating it in their childhood.

Greeks do not share the British acceptance of convenience foods so there were no tins, tubs or packets of halva pudding available in the shops. Eventually, I found this recipe and my grandsons and I enjoyed eating it.

½ cup of oil
½ cup of chopped walnuts
1 cup semolina
1 cup of water
1 cup sugar
1 cup of milk

Dissolve sugar in water and milk by bringing to boil and stirring. Brown semolina in heated oil, stirring constantly till golden brown. Add milk, water and walnuts. Mix and cook till it comes away at the sides. Spoon into buttered dish. It may be decorated with either cinnamon, nuts or cream or all three. It is best eaten fresh and warm. (But it does keep a little while in the freezer at a little cost to flavour.) If you have children around keeping it will not be a problem. It will all be eaten.

Naughty puddings

Sticky toffee pudding (serves four)

75g (3oz) margarine
50g (2oz) best soft dates, chopped
75g (3oz) Demerara
(or dark brown sugar)
1 tbsp milk
75g (3oz) SR flour
1 medium banana

For the glaze:

50g (2oz) light brown sugar
50g (2oz) butter
75g (3oz) double cream
(or just 4 tbsp syrup only)

Heat oven 200°C / 180°C fan / gas 6. Grease individual dishes. Mix glaze ingredients and spread on bottom of dish(es.) Cream fat and sugar. Gently beat in flour, banana, dates and milk. Bake for 20 minutes till springy in middle. Serve with cream or ice cream.

Toffee apple pudding: Use 2 tbsp of your best chunky homemade apple puree to replace banana.

Winter pudding (serves two)

This pudding is a great winter satisfier. As it is basically an egg custard watch that the oven is warm enough to set the egg but not hot enough for 'syneresis' to occur (tiny little holes).

40g butter *
65g sugar *
40g breadcrumbs – brown or white
85g dried cranberries *
1 egg, beaten
125g sultanas *
½ tsp cinnamon *
½ tsp nutmeg *
500ml milk *

Butter a ceramic dish (approx. 20cm x 15cm). Heat oven 170°C / 160°C fan / gas 3. Place starred ingredients in a pan and gently heat till butter melts. Remove from heat. Cool a little. Add breadcrumbs and egg. Tip into buttered baking dish and cover with foil.

Bake for about 40-45 minutes. Remove foil and cook another 15 minutes till golden brown and not wobbly. Serve hot or if serving cold, a tablespoon of white granulated sugar may be sprinkled on for a frost effect.

Date and brandy pudding (serves twelve)

In a rare moment of domestic thoroughness, I cleaned the top shelf of a hardly-used cupboard and came across some dates, pecan nuts, brown sugar and cherries. I told Stuart that I had no idea how they got there. To my astonishment he said that it was his surprise for me.

He had bought the ingredients to make an amazing pudding which he'd eaten on a business lunch. (This is a man who usually passes on desserts.) He had got the recipe, bought the main ingredients, hidden them and then forgotten all about it. I was amazed because he has no interest in cooking whatsoever.

I brought the ingredients down and put them on view to remind him to make it. When he did it was gorgeous. So gorgeous that he agreed to make it for one or two of the small dinner parties we all went in for in the 80's. It is an absolute winner.

Also it has to be cooked in advance which is useful when entertaining. It's not quick and easy but returns the effort tenfold.

200g (8oz) pitted dates
2 eggs, beaten
1 level tsp bicarbonate of soda
140g (5oz) self-raising flour
300ml (½ pint) boiling water
115g (4oz) chopped pecans / walnuts
100g (4oz) softened butter
115g (4oz) glacé cherries, chopped
225g (8oz) brown sugar

Heat oven 180°C / 160°C fan / gas 4 and butter lightly a shallow earthenware dish about 13 inches x 11 inches x 2¾ inches (33cm x 28cm x 7cm).

Brandy sauce:

225g (8oz) soft brown sugar
150ml (¼ pint) cold water
150ml (¼ pint) brandy

Mince the dates and place in a bowl with bicarbonate of soda. Pour over boiling water. In a bigger bowl, cream butter and sugar till fluffy and slowly beat in the eggs. Fold in the SR flour, nuts and cherries. Finally add the date mixture and bake for about 40 minutes. It is cooked if a skewer or small, sharp knife comes out clean and dry when pushed into the middle.

Gently warm the sauce ingredients over a low heat. Pour over the cooked pudding·and leave to cool. When ready to serve, heat through for about 15 minutes at 180°C / 160°C fan / gas 4. Accompany with vanilla ice cream or double cream, lightly whisked with a good pinch of ground nutmeg or cinnamon. Yum, yum!

Sam's tiramisu (serves six)

I believe tiramisu means 'pick-me-up.' It is essentially an Italian trifle and the good thing about trifles is, it's hard to get them wrong. As my husband passes on desserts, I was surprised to discover how much he likes this recipe, probably because it's bitter sweet and has two of his favourite ingredients.

200g (8oz) sponge fingers – about 20
250g mascarpone (tub)
10 fl oz strong coffee
8 tbsp of coffee liqueur eg Tia Maria
400g custard (tub)
(or make your own, see page 128)
2 tbsp cocoa
5 fl oz lightly whipped cream

Mix cooled coffee and liqueur in a jug. Place half the sponge fingers in a deep glass bowl. Pour over half the coffee mix and stand for 10 minutes. In a separate bowl, mix mascarpone and custard until smooth. Spread half over the sponge.

Dip remaining sponge fingers in the coffee mix and lay on top of the custard mix. Spread over rest of cheese mix. Chill for 2-3 hours. Cover with cream and sprinkle in cocoa. Chill for an hour.

Summer pudding

I love this pudding because it looks like a Christmas pudding, especially when glazed and its lighter texture and refreshing taste make it an attractive alternative to Christmas pudding. It is ridiculously easy to make.

6-8 trifle sponges (lightly cooked summer berries or a medium can of forest fruit)

for the glaze:
1 tbsp arrowroot blended with a little water and ¼ pint dark fruit juice

Line the pudding basin with sponges round the sides, then fill basin with fruit. Cover with sponges on top. Place a plate with a weight on top. Chill overnight. Turn onto a plate. That's it. Really.

If you wish to glaze it, blend arrowroot with a little water. Warm any leftover fruit juice on a low heat. Add blended arrowroot mix and bring to the boil stirring hard. The glaze thickens and becomes transparent and can be gently brushed over pudding enhancing its appearance.

Hazelnut and chocolate pudding (serves at least four)

A yummy dessert when served warm with cream. A gorgeous cake when cold. It also freezes well especially in slices which are quicker to thaw.

100g hazelnuts
1-2 tbsp chocolate & hazelnut spread
75g light muscovado sugar
pinch of salt
125g butter, thinly sliced
3 eggs
150g dark chocolate, broken up
double cream to serve

Heat oven to 220°C / 200°C fan / gas 7 and dry roast hazelnuts for about 5 minutes till golden. Take a moment to enjoy their magical aroma then remove any loose skins. Reduce oven to 180°C / 160°C fan / gas 4. Cool and chop nuts with knife or liquidiser till medium fine. Melt sugar, butter and chocolate in a pan over extremely low heat, stirring often.

Add chocolate spread and salt and cool. Whisk whites till they form soft peaks and stir yolks in chocolate mix if cool and add to whites. Gently fold together. Add hazelnuts. Pour into a greased and lined 20cm (8-inch) tin and bake for 35-40 minutes till dry to touch but wobbly beneath. Cool in tin. It may sink a little. Serve warm with cream. Enjoy the wonderful aroma of warm chocolate.

*

The introduction of the grey squirrel from America in the mid-19th century has made foraging hazelnuts an impossibility. The grey squirrel greedily gobbles them all up unripe, leaving none for our native reds – or us!

Rescued by Stuart, Chirpy lived in our lounge some months before he was ready for the wild. When settled in the woods, on hearing our call he crossed treetops to see us. An amazing experience.

Snowdon pudding (serves two easily)

Like Mississippi mud pie, there must be many explanations of the symbolic relationship twixt pudding and place in the name of this dessert. I think the topping or should I say the summit should look desirable so go for cherries and other glacé fruits on top.

I have adapted the more traditional steamed version to a simple microwavable sponge cake with glacé fruit added after cooking.

**2oz butter, chopped
2½ oz SR flour
2oz caster sugar
1 egg, beaten
1 lemon, zested and juiced
1-2 tbsp milk
handful of raisins**

Topping:
**2 tbsp syrup to drizzle over the warm cooked pudding
4 glacé cherries
2 crystallised stem ginger, chopped
a few slices of angelica to arrange on the summit**

Lightly butter a 1 pint microwave pudding bowl. Sieve the flour into a bowl and add sugar, egg, little lumps of butter. Beat well or whisk till smooth. Add lemon juice and zest and enough milk to make a soft batter. Pour into microwave basin, cling wrap top with the odd air hole puncture.

Microwave for 2 minutes when you'll probably see the mist descend. Stop. Allow steam to escape and continue in little blasts till pudding feels springy and shrinks from basin then remove. Stand a couple of minutes. Tickle syrup over and arrange glacé fruits seductively on top. I would serve with cream.

If you're doubling the recipe for hearty eaters, custard is a good choice. If trebling the recipe, steaming in a pan of water for 1½ hours may be easier. Microwaving, you'll need at least 4 minutes.

This pudding might easily be adapted to a ginger pudding, keep the raisins but use only chopped crystallised ginger on top and syrup to decorate. Another alternative is a topping of honey and walnuts.

English Afternoon tea

PICTURE a late afternoon in 1840. The Duchess of Bedford languishes in Woburn Abbey. Luncheon is a distant memory and dinner seems hours away. Yet chores must be faced like having to kiss the children goodnight, change for dinner and humour the butler by trying his cocktails at 6 o'clock.

Feeling peckish, the Duchess requests her butler to fetch a tray of tea and bread and butter, and English afternoon tea is born. It later became a national treat at about 4 o'clock for all classes. Sadly, the tea lady coming round the factory, office or staffroom with a trolley of tea, sandwiches and cake has gone despite its boost to morale and communication.

Restaurants have since revived it, often with a glass of bubbly alongside the teapot. At home, silverware and bone china are less fashionable but if you've got it, flaunt it. The Duchess was right about one thing, though, good homemade bread and butter and jam is often better than cake.

Plain soda bread

**250g white flour, strong or spelt
1 tsp bicarbonate of soda
250g wholemeal flour
400ml buttermilk or 450g live yogurt
1 tsp salt**

Heat oven to 200°C / 180°C fan / gas 6. In a big bowl mix dry ingredients and make a well for the buttermilk or yogurt. Mix in flour from sides till you have a sticky dough.

Shape into a ball and place on baking tray. Flatten to a depth of 7cm and score with sharp knife into four quarters. Bake about 40-45 minutes till it sounds hollow when tapped on the back.

Treacle can be used in soda bread recipes: as above with 450g flour, 50g oats, 1 tsp salt, 1 level tsp bicarbonate of soda, 1 tbsp treacle, 1 tbsp honey, 450ml buttermilk. Brush melted butter on the top when removed from oven.

Date and walnut soda bread

Plain soda bread is good but this is divine. It is fine alone or accompanied with cheese or apricot jam. Buttermilk may be replaced
by milk soured with a little lemon juice or live, natural yogurt.

450g mixed grain flour
1 tsp bicarbonate of soda
50g rolled oats
250ml buttermilk
50g walnuts, chopped or broken
200ml natural yogurt
100g pitted dates, chopped
1 tbsp honey
1 tsp salt

Oven 200°C / 180°C fan / gas 6. In a big bowl mix flour, salt, oats,
nuts, dates and bicarbonate of soda. Pour in milk, honey and
yogurt.

Quickly mix into a sticky dough and turn onto greased baking tray.
Shape into a round and cut deeply into quarters. Bake for 45-50
minutes till a hard, golden crust is formed. Remove to cool, brush-
ing top with melted butter.

Quick Spelt Bread

Spelt is an ancient wheat flour which is mainly interchangeable
with our modern, over-processed wheat flour but less processed
and therefore healthier.

White and brown spelt flour is available from supermarkets and
the brown flour has a lovely subtle nutty flavour.

As with all yeast cookery, remember that yeast is destroyed by
high temperatures but grows in the warmth of 29-30°C so a thermometer is essential for accuracy.

This ridiculously easy recipe benefits from the use of a black silicone oval bowl called a 'bread maker' which can be bought from
Lakeland. Fresh yeast may be bought from the bakery department
of most supermarkets where the bakers are very nice and helpful.

500g wholemeal spelt flour
400ml warm water (27-30°C)
½ tsp salt
1 tbsp honey
11g fresh yeast
(or 1 tsp quick dried yeast)
1 tbsp olive oil

Put black bowl on the scales. Add flour to weigh then stir in dried yeast if using and salt. Mix honey with warm water (30°C), crumble in the fresh yeast if using and stir to dissolve then add to dry ingredients. Add oil. (I like to add a few crushed walnuts and sometimes chopped dried figs too.)

Knead for a few minutes in the bowl or push it about with a spatula if you like to keep your hands clean. Leave to rise in a warm place (in the bowl) for about 25 minutes before baking 220°C / 200°C fan / gas 7 (in the bowl) for 40 minutes. Leave to cool on a rack. This bread is also delicious served with butter and homemade jam.

Perfect strawberry jam

Homemade, additive free strawberry jam tends to be runny. Once I daringly heated it beyond the setting point temperature and managed to produce concrete jam. Rather than throw it out, I would force it out of the jar even though the metal spoon bent.

Then I mixed it in the blender with a drop or two of boiling water. It worked. The consistency and taste were delicious.
The rest kept well in the jar as I had in effect concentrated it. Rather than have the bother of using a hammer and chisel, I now accept that strawberry jam may be runny and I follow the instructions exactly. I prefer to make two or three jars at a time.

4lb 6oz strawberries	or 2lb 3oz	or 1lb 1½ oz
4lb preserving sugar	2lb	1lb
juice of two lemons	1	½

Prepare jam jars by washing, rinsing and drying thoroughly, standing on a newspaper-lined baking tray in a low oven to dry them and keep them warm. Hull fruit. Set aside some whole strawberries and mash the rest. Put into pan, add sugar and lemon juice and bring to boil. Add rest of strawberries. Boil jam for 15 minutes. Stir regularly and in the last 5 minutes keep checking for setting point.

The three tests for setting point are: if you put a little jam on a chilled saucer, cool, then push it with a wooden spoon handle, it wrinkles if it is ready. Another test is to watch drops of jam fall from the wooden spoon when you stir. When the drops become flaky and sticking to the spoon it is done. Or use a thermometer and let it reach 104°C / 105°C.

(As explained earlier, homemade strawberry jam tends not to set as solidly as other jams but it is still gorgeous.) At setting point, remove from heat and skim off any scum. (A tiny knob of butter may disperse scum.) Cool slightly. Pour from a jug into warm jars. Cover with a disc of waxed paper. Seal with a cellophane top and store.

Delectable Damson Jam

Probably the best jam in the world and for foragers, the fruit is free. What a lovely sight a damson tree is in full fruit; its arching spindly branches so elegant bearing the black almond shaped fruit. Damsons are easy to pick and their stunning flavour is deep, rich and tangy.

Because of their stones, they are never quite satisfactory in a pie or crumble but damsons make great damson gin or jam or are tasty raw when ripe. Collecting them is a good excuse to get into woods at the start of their autumn glory, about mid-September.

Setting jam depends on a gum-like substance in fruit called pectin and the right proportion of acid and sugar. Damsons are rich in pectin and sugar, making it ideal for jam making.

- 5lb damsons are softened in water (about 1½ pints or less) before adding 6lb sugar. Yields 9-10lb.
- 1lb damsons are softened in water (about 6 fl oz) before adding 1.2lb sugar.

- 1 kg damsons are softened in water (about 450ml) before adding 1.25 kg sugar.

Wash, rinse, then dry jam jars in a low oven by standing upright. Keep warm. In a large pan lightly wash and stew fruit till soft. Add sugar, stir with a long handled wooden spoon. Bring to the boil fast. Continue to boil till setting point is reached, around 15 minutes, when the jam just starts sticking to the edge of the spoon.

Keep stirring throughout boiling to stop jam sticking to bottom of pan and a scum forming on top. Using a long-handled metal spoon, try picking out the rising stones from the surface WITHOUT GETTING BURNT. This is extreme jam making!

When ready according to tests highlighted above in strawberry jam method, have warm jars to hand. Carefully pour jam in a jug on the hob so no accidents possible. For safety, always work over a work surface. Pour jam into jars nearly to top. Cover with waxed disc and then cellophane cover.

> "Stands the church clock at ten to three.
> And is there honey still for tea."
>
> *Rupert Brooke*

Quick-dropped scones

Or are these Scotch or American pancakes? The difference is slight. This recipe freezes well and a slice heats up well from frozen, in the microwave or toaster. They are easy to make and only require that spoonfuls of batter are dropped onto a hot griddle or frying pan and they cook within minutes. Delicious with jam, cream and strawberries, especially when watching Wimbledon. I usually have three frying pans on the go to speed up the cooking of a batch. (For an American breakfast, mix the batter with blueberries.)

200g (½lb) spelt white flour with 3 level tsp baking powder
50g (2oz) golden caster sugar or syrup
50g (2oz) butter, margarine
1 egg
300ml (½ pint) milk
optional: 1-2oz currants or sultanas

Sieve flour and baking powder together into a mixing bowl. Rub fat into flour. Add beaten egg and enough milk, a bit at a time, to make a thick batter. Stir in fruit, then heat frying pan or griddle.

On a hot pan, drop a tablespoon of batter. Allow room for spreading before dropping next spoonful. When bubbles break on the surface of the cakes or the edges are darkening, flip cakes over.

Keep warm in a tea towel till all cooked. It's necessary with these types of scones or with pancakes to have the pan very hot whilst pouring on the batter and then reduce the heat to cook them through.

Victoria sandwich cake (serves two)

The classic Victoria sandwich cake knocked up in minutes.

50g (2oz) SR flour
(or plain with ¾ tsp baking
powder sieved in)
50g (2oz) caster sugar
50g (2oz) margarine
1 egg

Heat oven 200°C / 180°C fan / gas 6. Grease a small, slim loaf tin, say 22cm x 3½ cm x 7½ cm. Fold a double strip of baking / greaseproof paper to run the middle length of the tin and overlap the two short sides (for easy removal of the cake).

Place a small mixing bowl on the scales and put on zero. Weigh all the ingredients one at a time. Whisk briefly together till united. Add any special flavouring eg coffee essence now. Pour into prepared tin and bake 20-25 minutes or more till golden and springy in the middle when tested with a finger. Cool.

Flavour as you please, for example:

Strawberry cream: coat top with thick or whisked double cream. Decorate with fresh strawberries.

Lemon drizzle: Add grated rind of one lemon to cake mix before baking. Put skewer holes in cooled cake. Mix an equal amount of granulated sugar with lemon juice (about a tbsp each) and pour over top a bit at a time to make a gritty topping. (My daughter says this is the best lemon drizzle cake in the world.)

Welsh cakes

200g flour
100g butter
75g caster sugar, more for dusting
1 egg, beaten
40g currants

Add sugar to flour and rub butter into it until it is like fine bread-crumbs. Add currants then beat in egg. The mixture should be firm enough to draw together, with fingers, like pastry. (Add a little milk if it feels too dry.)

Roll out till 5mm thick and cut into rounds with a fluted cutter. Heat a frying pan or griddle and cook cakes a couple of minutes on both sides. Remove and dust with caster sugar. Delicious. For an extra treat serve with a dollop of extra thick cream and a strawberry on top.

Best bara brith

Bara brith is Welsh for speckled bread. Versions vary from a rather plain loaf with a few currants here and there to a rich fruit cake. This recipe hits it just right.

It slices well, freezes well and doesn't need to be buttered unless you've had a really bad day trying to call the tax office or getting a doctor's appointment or the blinds you ordered are the wrong colour. I love the fact that it has tea and marmalade in it. It all seems very British.

Overnight: **soak 250g-300g (10-12oz) dried fruit in 16 fl oz tea and keep overnight.**

Next morning: strain fruit and place into a large bowl to which all the other ingredients are added and well mixed. Keep the liquor.

To fruit add:

> **75g (3oz) sugar**
> **1 large egg**
> **2 tbsp marmalade**
> **300g (12oz) plain white flour**
> **or spelt white flour sieved with**
> **4½ tsp baking powder**
> **1 tsp mixed spice or more**

(If using SR flour use ½ tsp baking powder). Mix in enough left over fruit liquor to make a soft dropping consistency and bake in two lined pound loaf tins at 170°C / 150°C fan / gas 3-4 for 40 minutes. It is cooked when a skewer inserted in the middle comes out clean.

Boiled British fruit cake
_____

No more tennis elbow trying to cream the butter with the sugar. Boiled fruit cake is easier to make and gives a better result. Before it even gets in the oven, the toffee smell filling the house is fabulous. Win, win!

300g (12oz) mixed dried fruit (nice if some of it is chopped dates and walnuts)
25g (1oz) chopped cherries, tossed in some of the flour
150g (6oz) butter, cut in lumps
175g (7oz) dark brown soft sugar
1 full tsp mixed spice and pinch cinnamon
175g (7oz) SR flour
2 eggs, beaten
a handful of broken walnuts for the top

Place mixed fruit in pan, cover with water, boil and simmer for 5 minutes. Pour water off. Stir in butter, then sugar, cherries, walnuts, flour and spices. When mix is cool, add eggs.

Pour into 2 lined loaf tins, about 9cm x 21cm x 6cm. Place halved walnuts on top if desired. Bake at 180°C / 160°C fan / gas 4 for about 50 mins till a skewer in the middle comes out clean. Cool. Slice. Butter and enjoy!

A slice of good fruit cake and a cup of tea is so therapeutic and comforting, all counsellors should serve it just like headmasters should have sherry in their filing cabinet.

Carrot cake

100g (4oz) wholemeal spelt flour,
sieved with 1½ tsp baking powder,
½ tsp ground ginger; ½ tsp cinnamon
100g (4oz) light brown sugar
25g (1oz) chopped walnuts (optional)
100g (4oz) margarine
50g (2oz) sultanas
3 eggs, beaten
2 carrots, grated
7-inch cake tin, greased and lined
1 tbsp orange juice
120g cream cheese

Preheat oven to 190°C / 170-180°C fan / gas 5. In a basin mix the flour, sugar, margarine and eggs before folding in the sultanas, walnuts and carrots. Spread in tin and bake 30-40 minutes till firm and springy in middle. Remove. Stand for 10 minutes, turn out and cool. For topping mix cream cheese with orange juice and spread over cake.

Orange and almond cake

300g ground almonds
5 eggs
250g granulated sugar
200ml sunflower oil
2 tsp baking powder
2 tsp agave nectar
zest from 2 oranges
glaze: 3 tbsp flaked almonds, lightly crushed
2-3 tbsp sugar
juice from 2 oranges

20cm / 8-inch cake tin, greased. Oven 180°C / gas 4. Mix together
the ground almonds, sugar and baking powder. In a separate bowl
whisk together the eggs, sunflower oil, 2 tsp agave nectar and the
fruit zest. Combine the two mixtures. Pour into tin and bake for
35-40 minutes till an inserted skewer in the middle comes out
clean. Allow to cool a little and carefully turn onto a plate.

To make glaze: mix orange juice with 2 tbsp sugar and lightly
crushed, flaked almonds. Drizzle over cake. If it does not all
absorb, keep and drizzle more over later. Serve plain as a cake or
with cream as a pudding.

Chocolate beetroot buns

If cooking for suspicious folk, do not mention the word beetroot.
They won't notice. Depending on many factors like size of cake
cases and humidity, these buns come out slightly different every
time I make them but they are always delicious unless you have
not weaned yourself off highly-sweetened cakes that many shops
serve and research shows contain staggering amounts of sugar.

At the time of writing, Pret a Manger's lemon drizzle slice has 18
teaspoons of sugar, Starbucks' carrot cake 15 teaspoons and Costa
Coffee's 14 teaspoons per cake. Good reasons to make your own
cakes.

**200g cooked beetroot
3 medium eggs
200g best dark 70% cocoa chocolate
and a further 100g for icing
juice & finely grated zest of an orange
125g golden caster sugar
100g almonds
½ tsp baking powder**

Heat oven 190°C / 170°C / gas 5. Melt chocolate in a heatproof
bowl over hot water and then cool a little. Puree beetroot and in a
bowl stir in orange juice and zest. Add almonds, baking powder
and melted chocolate. Whisk eggs with sugar and when thick fold
in cake mixture. Spoon mixture into cake cases and bake for 20-25
minutes. Ice with remaining melted chocolate.

Quick chocolate sponge cake

**100g (4oz) plain flour
1 egg
150g (6oz) caster sugar
4½ fl oz milk
¾ tsp baking powder
2 fl oz veg oil
¾ tsp bicarbonate of soda
1 tsp vanilla extract
75g (3oz) cocoa powder
4½ fl oz boiling water**

optional: **top with walnuts before icing sets**

Heat oven 180°C / 160°C fan / gas 4. Line 20cm (8-inch) sandwich tin. Place all dry ingredients in a bowl and beat in milk, eggs, oil and vanilla extract. A bit at a time, beat in boiling water. Pour this liquid batter into the lined tin and bake 25-30 minutes or until the top is springy. Cool.

Make icing either (a) sweet and glossy or (b) fudgy:

a) sweet and glossy:

**150g (6oz) icing sugar
1 tbsp cocoa
pinch cinnamon and all spice,
all blended with a little water
small knob of butter
1-2 tbsp hot water**

Sieve icing sugar into a bowl. Blend cocoa and spice with a little water. In a pan on a low heat melt butter with 1-2 tbsp hot water. Add blended cocoa. Beat till smooth. Turn off heat and stir in icing sugar slowly. Add more warm water if needed. The icing should coat the back of the spoon and be warm not hot. Ice cake.

b) fudgy:
Melt 200g (8oz) plain chocolate in a bowl over hot water. Remove. Whisk in same amount of double cream till thick. Spread over cake. *Nice for afternoon tea:* the cake freezes well, especially in slices and thaws quickly before the tea has brewed.

Hazelnut and chocolate cake

The hazelnut and chocolate pudding on page 138 makes a gorgeous cake when served cold and sliced.

"Pleasure is a nutrient."

Fairy cakes

Whatever happened to fairy cakes? Those dainty tasty little sponge cakes. Who decided they would mutate into giant sickly 'muffins? Actually I know who. That American salesman in the Fifties who when told to increase the sales of popcorn at a cinema, found a simple solution. He increased the portions. This trick of capitalist exploitation has now caught on everywhere.

Often it is difficult to get a small coffee or a small or medium anything in motorway cafés or most places. However, sharing a meal is becoming accepted practice even in America where I noticed recently waiters are happy to bring you an extra plate and cutlery.

What worries me is that a whole generation has grown up in the UK, not knowing what an appropriate portion of food or drink is.

100g (4oz) soft margarine
handful of either currants, raisins
or sultanas
2 eggs
100g (4oz) caster sugar
100g (4oz) SR flour
add 2½ tsp baking powder with spelt
or plain flour

Heat oven 200°C / 180°C fan / gas 6. Mix all the ingredients together with a wooden spoon and a strong right arm. You can use an electric whisk but it's not the same as licking a spoon afterwards! (If you do lick the whisk, turn off the electricity first.).

Spoon a generous teaspoon of mixture into proper, old-fashioned dainty cake cases on a bun tin and bake for 20 minutes until springy in the middle.

Quick Florentines

These taste as good as the original Florentine biscuits but are much less fiddly. The worst part is getting out the ingredients. If I do this a day or two before, the sight of them prompts me to make them and the whole operation is quicker.

150g (6oz) dark chocolate
a pinch of salt
100g (4oz) condensed milk
62g (2½ oz) glacé cherries, chopped
137g (5½ oz) mixed fruit
(cranberries, raisins, mixed peel)
87g (3½ oz) chopped nuts
25g (1oz) sunflower seeds

Grease two Swiss roll tins (30cm x 23cm x 4cm) and line with buttered greaseproof paper. Heat oven to 180°C / 160°C fan / gas 4. Next melt chocolate in a bowl over a pan of water. Spread over tin and chill one hour. Mix condensed milk, fruit, salt and nuts. Spread over the chocolate layer and bake for 15-17 minutes till firm.

Whilst cooling mark into small squares. Refrigerate two hours then turn out. (Use up condensed milk by whisking with 10oz double cream and rind and juice of 3 lemons for a quick mousse.)

Pecan cookies

When you get a sugar urge, these are quicker to make than walking to the corner shop and they taste so much better than bought biscuits. I once made them with wholemeal spelt flour by mistake and they were just as tasty.

75g butter (or margarine)
115g white spelt flour sieved with
¼ tsp baking powder
75g caster sugar
12 pecan nuts

Turn oven on to 190°C / 170°C fan / gas 5. Cream together fat and sugar. Mix in flour to make a soft dough. Using hands roll into

12 -14 balls. Place each ball well apart on a greased baking tray
and press a nut on top of each. Bake 12-15 minutes till golden.
Then, carefully but quickly transfer to a wire cooling tray.

Microwaved meringues

These cakes are a godsend as the paste keeps for ages allowing
you to freshly bake four at a time in seconds. It's fun watching
them expand in the microwave. Okay, they contain a lot of sugar
but you only need eat one small one topped with cream and a
strawberry.

I find this approach to food preferable to self-denial. There is no
pressure to eat more as the cooked meringues keep well in an airtight container too. My grandsons were ecstatic about them especially, being allowed to squirt cream on, accompanied by my
screaming, 'That's enough!'

Perhaps it was beginner's luck but the first ones I made came out
perfect. Subsequently, I struggled to get the size and cooking right
and ended up incinerating the one in the middle. However, I now
get consistently perfect results with the following method.

1 small egg white (15g) lightly beaten
5oz (150g) icing sugar

To the egg white add sifted sugar. Don't whisk but mix with a
wooden spoon. Knead till it is a pliable, smooth mix that can be
rolled into balls. It's usually right when the gloss goes off the mix.
Divide into balls about the size of a 10p and weighing 10g each.
(The weight is crucial.)

Line the microwave turntable with greaseproof paper, (the greaseproof paper is also crucial) or you can use a very flat plastic plate.

Place on 4 balls or flattened discs at a time, well separated in a
ring. Microwave for 50 seconds in an 800w oven. Remove
carefully with a fish slice. Fill with cream and fruit or nuts. Any
damaged ones can be mixed into whisked double cream and
strawberries for an Eton Mess. Leftovers keep for many days in an
airtight tin.

"The meringues were large and white and brittle as coral and stuffed to overflowing with cream."

Gerald Durrell's The Corfu Trilogy

By the time the meringues appear, fourteen-year-old Gerald has eaten soup, 'little' fish, snipe, wild boar and a shrimp omelette accompanied by champagne, brandy, white wine, red wine 'dark as the heart of a dragon.' On his way home from the Countess' lunch, he is 'deliciously and flamboyantly sick.'

Anzac biscuits

Eaten on the day of remembrance for Australian and New Zealand Army Corps. I have a problem with these biscuits – I can't stop eating them!

> **85g oats**
> **85g desiccated coconut**
> **100g plain flour**
> **100g white sugar**
> **100g butter**
> **2 tbsp syrup**

Place mixing bowl on scales, turn on. Weigh dry ingredients. Heat oven 180°C / 160°C fan / gas 4. Line or grease two large baking trays. Melt butter and syrup slowly in a pan. In a little bowl, measure 1 tsp bicarbonate of soda.

Add 1 tbsp boiling water and pour onto the bicarbonate of soda. It should froth. Add frothing soda to the syrup butter mix then pour mix into well of all the dry ingredients combined and gently stir together. It should be a sticky, soft batter.

Place dessertspoon dollops onto tray an inch apart, about eight altogether and bake on each tray, a total of about 22 biscuits. Flatten them and bake 10 minutes till golden brown. Enjoy the aroma filling the house whilst washing up and getting the wire cooling rack out.

This recipe only just squeezed into my collection as the biscuits spread in the oven, creating more washing up of baking trays than is usually tolerable.

Also, the first time I made them the bicarbonate was old and didn't froth, which made great brandy snaps: tasty, but not what I wanted. I now buy bicarbonate of soda in sachets so it stays fresh and active. You can always halve the recipe and only have one baking tray to wash.

Traditional Teas and Tisanes

As the British know, to make good tea, first warm the pot. Drain. Into the pot place a tsp of loose tea per person and one for the pot. Pour on boiling water. Curiously, our continental friends seem not to grasp the importance of pouring boiling water on tea leaves. Tepid will not do.

The tea most often served at The Ritz, London, for afternoon tea is Earl Grey, taken with or without milk. It is a black Indian tea fused with bergamot. If you prefer a robust taste, try Kenyan breakfast tea. Most people's every-day cuppa is made from a blend of black tea leaves from India or Africa.

Taylors make a gorgeous black tea with dried rose petals. It's delicious and delicate. (Just right for a garden party if that's your thing.) If the blend of tea is old, health benefits may be lost.

Reputable tea companies are more likely to sell fresher tea leaves probably from one source. Bear in mind, black, green and white teas contain caffeine and also tannins which may become bitter if steeped longer than 3-4 minutes.

Teatime camping in the back garden with Edna, George, mother and me.
Greenbank Gardens, 1954.

Herbal Teas

Herbal teas do not contain caffeine or tannin so you can steep for as long as you like. In Crete where longevity reigns, tea is made from dried Cretan mountain herbs and the health benefits are said to be amazing. Perhaps that is the secret of how Ancient Greece produced such great thinkers. Aristotle liked his cuppa.

Our English herbs make lovely drinks too and are made like ordinary tea. Wash the herbs and warm the teapot. Fling in a small handful of leaves. Pour over boiling water and allow to infuse for 2-5 minutes.

Try:

Mint	The tangy freshness is said to aid digestion.
Fennel	The aniseed taste soothes an upset tummy.
Camomile	Calms & aids sleep, as Peter Rabbit's mother knew.
Tarragon	It has a liquorice flavour.
Borage	There is a honey taste.
Parsley	Aids digestion and is fresh and clean to taste.
Peppermint	It is said to be calming.

A combination of the leaves of borage, ginger, lemon balm and thyme can be used with any of the above to create a great taste. Turmeric, used in Indian and Ayurvedic medicine for hundreds of years, is the latest super food and great medicinal claims are made for it.

Drink daily and before you know it you'll be tying your feet round your head, should you wish to. If you cannot grow herbs in your garden, the shop-bought ones may keep well if watered daily and placed in the light of a window ledge.

Ginger and mint reviver

one inch of fresh ginger
8 mint leaves, lightly washed

Peel ginger and thinly slice into 10-12 pieces. Place in teapot with mint leaves and enough boiling water for two cups, (it is so good you'll want two cups). Infuse 2-3 minutes. Enjoy the flavour and the satisfaction of making real tea.

Lemon balm and fennel: wash fresh leaves briefly. Discard stalks of fennel and place leaves in pot.

Turmeric tea: Per cup, mix 1 tsp turmeric powder and 1 tsp honey before pouring on nearly boiling water. Use black pepper (as it helps in absorption) and lemon juice to flavour.

After-Dinner Treats

Irish Coffee

THIS divine drink has caught on around the world. When dining out with my brother at Gummies in Cape Town, the owner would appear at the end of the meal with a trayful of Irish Coffees, perfectly made in old fashioned classic wine glasses.

They looked and tasted gorgeous and were on the house. Now there's a man who knows how to treat his guests!

Making Irish coffee is a challenge. Some people cheat by squirting on pressured cream as it floats more easily but it doesn't taste or look quite as good as fresh cream. Do not worry if it ends up looking like coffee rather than Guinness. It will still taste sublime.

Per person:
Freshly-made ground coffee (arabica is the best), a sugar cube or teaspoon of brown sugar, whisked double cream that is still pourable, and a generous teaspoon of whiskey.

Strong glasses should first be warmed up with hot water. Place sugar in warm glass. (This is one of those times when sugar is essential.) Add a little hot coffee to dissolve sugar, stir well then fill glass two-thirds full. Add whiskey. Set a teaspoon to touch inside edge of glass. Pour cream to flow widely and slowly over the back of the teaspoon onto the surface of coffee without sinking it.

Petits fours: These simple sweets, which children of all ages enjoy creating, make tasty gifts at Christmas.

Coconut ice

	75g desiccated coconut
	150g icing sugar
optional:	**2 tbsp condensed milk**
	drop of pink colouring

Mix together condensed milk and icing sugar. Stir in coconut.

Mixture should be very stiff. Either roll into sweet size balls or divide into 2 identical bars and tint one pink and press bars together. Leave to set on a plate of dusted icing sugar. (For an Indian flavour add a dash of cinnamon and/or cardamom powder.)

Peppermint creams

1 egg white
200g icing sugar
1dssp lemon juice
dash of peppermint flavouring

Beat egg white lightly. Sieve icing sugar and add to white. Add the lemon juice, then a dash of peppermint flavouring. Beat till firm, roll out and cut into small rounds.

Stuffed Dates

Almond paste made by mixing:

200g ground almonds
100g sieved icing sugar
100g caster sugar
1 yolk or half a beaten egg
drop of vanilla
drop of almond essence

Stone the dates and slit open. Stuff with almond paste and put in sweet cases.

Almond paste balls: Make paste as above and shape into long rolls. Cut equal-sized pieces to shape into balls. Place ginger or walnuts on top.

Truffles

50g butter
2 tsp sieved cocoa or cacao
50g caster sugar
50g cake crumbs (or trifle sponge)
75g ground almonds
almond essence

Mix butter, sugar and almonds together to form a stiff peak. Add cocoa and crumbs and beat well. Flavour with almond essence or with rum, sherry or orange juice by kneading. Shape into balls and dust with cocoa or sieved icing sugar.

A final thought

Eating can be a joy and it should be one of life's fundamental pleasures. But the best food in the world is indigestible to those who are shocked, traumatised or miserable. It helps to feel at peace and harmony with the world.

"Unquiet meals make ill digestions."

Shakespeare's Comedy of Errors

A Seasonal Calendar

	In the shops	In the fields	In the kitchen	In the diary
Jan	Clementines, Seville oranges, leek, parsnips, kale, spinach, swede, celeriac		Soups, stews, pies, roasts, hearty puddings, marmalade making	Burns' Night Supper, 25th
Feb	As above, oranges, lemons, cauliflower, kale, leeks, swede		Leek and potato soup, cauliflower cheese	Shrove Tuesday, Valentine's Dinner, 14th
Mar	Sprouts, spring cabbage, kale, cauliflower, leeks, prunes		Roast shoulder or leg of lamb, hotpots, stews	St David's Day Dinner, 1st, St Patrick's Dinner, 17th
Apr	Broccoli, spring cabbage, cauliflower, peas, radishes, rhubarb, Jersey potatoes	St George's mushrooms, wild garlic, champignons	Jersey potatoes with roast lamb, chocolate puddings, vegetable soup	Easter Sunday, St George's Day, 23rd
May	Bananas, dates, cabbage, spinach, peas, Jersey potatoes, broccoli, early strawberries	Wild garlic, watercress, nettles	Kebabs, steaks, salads, baked bananas, gooseberry fool	May 1st celebrations, May Day Bank Holiday
Jun	Carrots, cauliflowers, beans, aubergines, salad veg, peas, raspberries, nectarines, peaches	Basil, thyme, dulse, samphire, puff balls, elderflowers	Salads and steaks, esp salmon, Summer pudding, asparagus, baked bananas, gooseberry fool	Wimbledon build-up
Jul	French, broad and runner beans, celery, new potatoes, figs, cherries, strawberries	As above plus bilberries and cherries	Asparagus, fresh mackerel, crab, light soups, peas and watercress	Picnic concerts

	In the shops	In the fields	In the kitchen	In the diary
Aug	All green beans, celery	Field mushrooms	Barbecues, picnics, foreign fare	Start of the grouse season
Sep	British fruits and veg, game season	Blackberries, plums, apples, pears, damsons, elderberries, field mushrooms	Pickling, bottling, making jams and jellies, wine and chutney, poached pears	Back to school
Oct	Broccoli, sprouts, red cabbage, Carrots	Fungi, nuts, crab apples, rosehips, figs	Soups, stews, roasts, pickling, braised cabbage	Halloween, October 31st
Nov	Pumpkins, squash, sprouts		Make Christmas pudding	Bonfire night, 5th, Remembrance Day, 11th
Dec	Cranberries, sprouts, swede	Holly, ivy, mistletoe, laurel	Make and freeze cranberry sauce, bread sauce, decorate cake, make mince pies	Christmas Day, 25th, New Year's Eve, 31st

Diary of an English Year

January 25th Burns Supper

Burns Cottage, birthplace of Scotland's greatest poet and probably the world's most successful. Ayr, 2009.

THE last leaf has fallen and the woods are dreary, damp and dark. What better time to don some cheerful tartan, harness your bagpipes and pay homage to Scotland's most famous poet. A party at this time of year is very welcome and a simple formula is:

- smoked salmon starters
- haggis with cranberry sauce and neeps and tatties (turnips and potatoes)
- cranach pudding (a Scottish oats syllabub)

A Scottish singsong round the fire and a short quiz adds to the fun. One year, it snowed heavily at our Burns party and a couple left early. They called next day to say they had to abandon their car in a snowdrift but after an enchanting walk beneath starry skies and over fresh, crunchy snow they managed to find a pub.

Ben, tall with red hair, and a snow-crested long beard by then, was still wearing his kilt whilst Pat had kept warm by donning a

Father Christmas outfit, which being a play group leader, she just happened to have in the car.

When they finally found 'The Fox and Hounds', it was laughter and applause all round from the locals at the sight of Father Christmas and Rob Roy and whisky all round from the Landlord. Sometime later, they were reluctantly rescued on what was described as the best night of their lives.

February / March Shrove Tuesday (Mardi Gras)

This moveable feast, based on the cycles of the moon, is still observed in many cultures. It necessitates the eating up of rich ingredients by making food such as pancakes, doughnuts or sweet pastries, ready to start a fast for Lent the next day. To me and my big brother George, it was just about eating as many pancakes as possible and therefore one of the best days of the year.

At four o'clock, we would run the mile home from St Thomas' Primary school alongside the Manchester Ship Canal to Greenbank Gardens, up the garden path, through the French window and straight to the kitchen where Mum's large yellow bowl was waiting for us, full of batter.

Though she was only inches away on the other side of the door, we knew never to disturb her whilst she was attending a client. Sometimes the phone would ring for her and I was taught to answer that she was in the saloon. (Only years later did I realise why this raised a chuckle.) For George, cooking or more precisely, eating, was and still is, his biggest passion. Blazers off, I was sitting on a high stool to watch his pancake demonstration.

Mum's classic batter:	*George's perfect pancakes:*
200g flour	**250ml batter**
2 eggs	**1-2 lemons**
500 ml of milk	**100g granulated sugar**
oil (we used lard back then)	**pinch of salt**

Sieve flour into bowl (we never had a sieve) and make a well in the middle into which the egg is cracked and half the milk added. Beat with a wooden spoon drawing the flour in gradually from the sides until it makes the sound of galloping horses. Slowly mix in the rest of the milk. It is desirable but not essential to leave the

batter to stand. This softens the gluten. Stir batter and pour some
into a jug. Melt a small lump of lard or use enough oil to coat the
pan, pouring off excess into a cup. Heat the oil until a tiny whisper
of blue smoke appears. (Pan must be very hot.)

With your weaker left hand, lift pan from heat and with your right
pour in just enough batter whilst manoeuvring the pan to thinly
coat the base and set on contact. This dextrous move requires
practice. Turn heat low. Watch for a minute or two.

*

At this point George would fold his arms and converse with me,
perhaps about how the recent sinking of The Mary P. Cooper in
the Manchester Ship Canal had caused the chaos Hitler had tried
but failed to do or how our bread man who we thought had been
attacked and robbed in the backs (as it was known) had done it to
himself with razors and was going to prison or how big sister
Edna's courtship with Wilf, head choirboy, was over now that
Mum knew that Wilf had shoved George's fireworks down a drain
after he caught George sneaking them into church under his
surplice.
    Oh yes, that Wilf had a lot to answer for, wasting money like
that. Her hard-earned money from the saloon.
*

Notice when the edges of the pancake curl. That's the time to give
the pan a shake to make sure it is loose. Next you either just flip it
over with a palette knife (which we didn't have) or go for the
exhilaration of tossing it high in the air and trying to catch it.

When it is caught or scraped off wherever it lands, the flip side is
briefly cooked till golden brown, tipped onto a sugared plate,
rolled up and covered in freshly squeezed lemon juice and pre-
sented, in this case to me. Delicious. I wondered why we never ate
pancakes or lemons at any other time of the year. I suppose Mum
was busy with her clients.

*

George won our pancake eating contest 6-3. He'd been in train-
ing with Tony next door. Tony went on to become the new pie-
eating champion of Lymm Rugby Club, beating his rival 22- 17.
When Tony was asked why he didn't stop at 18, he replied, 'I was

hungry.' At home George won all our contests like Snakes and ladders and poker by changing the rules as he went along (floating black twos in poker?).

His wife, Cathy, insists that he still does this on the golf course today. Talking about golf, George used to slip out of games on a Wednesday afternoon at Lymm Grammar to go fishing, taking a short cut across the golf course, rod in hand.

One day he came face to face with the Headmaster in his plus fours about to tee off. With nowhere to hide he prepared himself for a telling off and said, 'Hello Sir' to which the Head replied in a flat, airy tone without taking his eye off his golf ball but miming his swing, 'I haven't seen you Glover . . . and you . . . haven't seen me.' And that was the end of it. I'm not sure whether they continued to meet and ignore each other.

*

Pancakes make good savoury wraps for lunch or for a lasagne style dinner dish with a filling of tuna, prawns or chicken in cheese sauce or a Bolognese mince sauce and a cheese sauce on top, known as toreador pancakes. They freeze well rolled up ready for a quick meal another day. (Note to self: you might get more adventurous with your pancakes and make the delicious Staffordshire oatcake variety.)

February 14th Valentine's Day

Valentine's Day is a good excuse to dine out though some men like to cook for their woman. I would find that strange. But then my husband is a complete stranger to the kitchen though not to romance.

The funniest and truest card he ever sent me said, 'It's your birthday: sit back, relax and let me take care of everything. By the way, where is everything?' So of course, I appreciate a meal out. It is more romantic without the panic, steam, smells and worries of the kitchen.

But even in a restaurant, most likely abroad, a gypsy fiddler comes round or a Mexican trio and because of your enthusiasm for live music and approving smile, they come to your table and won't go away (even after a tip) and it doesn't seem polite to eat whilst they are playing so your meal gets cold and your smile fades. I conclude that live music and dining are best enjoyed separately.

On Valentine's day, restaurants now compete with romantic-sounding menus but dishes you might make yourself, if you are so inclined, are:

- passion fruit cocktail
- fiery steak with fresh green salad and sweet potatoes
- rose petal prosecco jelly or bee my honey pudding

Much to the amusement of his colleagues and their partners, that's from left to right, me, Graham, Mary, Sue and my husband Stuart, a monocled John Croft toasts the Empire. Oswestry School, Valentine Ball, 2005.

March 1st St David's Day

This day coincides with the appearance of leeks and daffodils, the emblems of Wales. In Shakespeare's Henry V, after the battle of Agincourt, Fluellen says, 'Wearing leeks is an honourable badge of service' to which Henry replies, 'I wear it. I am Welsh you know.' Think about that.

Our greatest soldier king was Welsh and he or rather his young French widow, Catherine de Valois, started the great Tudor dynasty following her affair with Owen Tudor, keeper of the Queen's closet or silver stick in waiting or something.

Many years later, the Tudor dynasty ended with the reign of our greatest British monarch ever, Elizabeth I. Good reasons to celebrate the Welsh.

Saint David's Day Supper

- Menai mussels
- Welsh lamb chops or Glamorgan sausages or 'sewin' (sea trout) with leeks in cheese sauce
- Snowdon pudding

March 17th St Patrick's Day

The Irish have a wonderful humour. Only they could invent an instrument that can be played whilst drinking: the Irish Pipes.

Their music is soulful, joyful and completely life affirming. We visited Dublin on this special day and enjoyed perfect Guinness while listening to the traditional music in Fitzsimmons, Temple Bar.

I saw the lady next to me wipe away a tear. She told me that she had to leave to catch her plane to Canada,' adding emphatically, 'I don't want to go.' She was sober unlike the passenger on the ferry home that night who was intermittently snoozing then waking up in the middle of the Irish Sea and shouting, 'Somebody get me a taxi, a taxi . . .'

Anyway, if you can't get to Ireland on this special day, play the Chieftains at home and serve a supper like:

- Smoked salmon with soda bread
- Beef in Guinness casserole or bacon and barley stew
- Bailey's flavoured tiramisu or Bailey's topped ice cream
- Irish coffee

April 23rd St George's Day

The patron saint of England's day is not much celebrated. In fact many English people are unaware of it. Unlike our Celtic neighbours we are either embarrassed about displays of national pride or perhaps so confident as a nation that we don't feel the need.

But this day is also recognised as Shakespeare's birthday so why not go in for a quintessential Elizabethan English Dinner:

- a glass of sack or porter wine
- roast Beef of Olde England with Yorkshire pudding, roast potatoes and seasonal vegetables
- syllabub or sherry trifle

Easter

To my parents, Easter meant the beginning of the caravan and camping season. Our first caravan was bought from a local farmer who had kept chickens in it. Brother George tells me that he and Dad cleaned it (many times) before painting it sky blue.

The cleaned-up caravan, Llanddulas, 1960.

Mum upholstered the seating in a tapestry fabric, piping the edges and adding to the comfort with her crimson velvet curtains. It was placed in a field near Gwrych Castle, far from the madding crowds of Rhyl where we used to holiday when I was an infant. Eager to enjoy its delights and no doubt to get as much value as possible from the ground rent, we arrived at Easter in snow or rain but never sunshine.

It was often freezing outside and frosty within as Mum and Dad were exhausted from managing their businesses. George remained the eternal happy camper, away from dawn to dusk, coming home at night with fish and game for Mum to cook. I enjoyed the rabbit stew but passed on the eels and anything fishy.

My happiest memory is of being very cosy in bed at night, all of us listening to the Radio 4 bedtime story. We did have good times at the caravan but not usually at Easter.

Easter Sunday celebrates the resurrection of Jesus and traditionally involves the slaying of a lamb. Thank goodness George was ignorant of this. He would have relished it. Poor lamb. A more palatable custom is the boiling of eggs or the painting of them, as symbols of spring and re-birth.

These days, chocolate eggs and chocolate desserts are the favourite. Whilst a little dark chocolate is good for you, some desserts like Death by Chocolate (the clue's in the title), chocolate fudge cake or chocolate cheesecake are not. The desserts suggested below should not make you feel sick all afternoon.

A traditional Easter lunch:

- roast lamb with mint sauce and gravy, fresh peas and roast potatoes
- poached seasonal rhubarb with ginger flavoured cream or chocolate mousse (made with avocados) or poached bananas with chocolate sauce

May 1st

Don't call the police if on your village green you see white-trousered men with little bells round their shins, walking and sometimes breaking into a skip whilst waving handkerchiefs and sticks. They are Morris men re-enacting ancient fertility rites. They should be employed before international rugby matches as an answer to the All Blacks and their haka.

Think how this display of manhood to the music of the floral dance would strike terror in the opposition as the bagpipes did in the Battle of Culloden.

The All Blacks would be so beguiled that it would be 10-0 to England before they knew it. I'm surprised nobody has thought of this before, especially Monty Python.

May should be a time of sunshine and blooming meadows: time for picnics. Picnics are simple, cheap and keep you out of doors as long as possible. The casual, 'ready in a jiff' picnic is often preferable to a mediocre meal out.

To be stuck somewhere without sustenance for any length of time was torture for my little family so I acquired the habit of packing water and sandwiches, along with bathing costumes, sunglasses, mac and umbrella, wherever we went. Just throw buns, butter and ham or cheese into a basket along with a chopping board.

With a butter spreading knife you can make lunch anywhere. Add picnic plates, serviettes, fruit and a bottle of water each. If the ideal meadow with a spreading chestnut tree or a golden, isolated beach cannot be found or it rains, the picnic may be eaten in the car which is cheaper and less stressful than searching miles for a decent pub.

My picnic hamper, a light straw affair with two long handles, lives by the front door, ready for action.

A picnic in the meadow with Katy, Michael, baby Bonnie and me.
Little Pentre, 1988.

My Dad's Picnic

Lack of money in my childhood was never a reason for us not to get out and about. First it was on the child's seat of my Dad's bike to Walton Park with its rolling lawns, swings, aviary and a bandstand where in times past Dad and his brothers would have played.

Bicycles were followed by cars: an Austin Seven, a Rover 141, and then a green Austin A35 van. Fort Perch Rock at Wallasey was a popular destination as were picturesque Cheshire villages like Great Budworth. Most vivid is the memory of my Dad taking his Primus stove up the Great Orme at Llandudno to warm up a tin of peas.

George says we had pea sandwiches and they were delicious. I remember we rose to chicken on occasions though never again after a seagull stole Dad's chicken leg from his hand and swallowed it whole a few yards in front of him. It was back to pea butties after that.

June 21ˢᵗ Midsummer Day

As a child, my birthday in late June coincided with Warrington Walking Day, a religious festival where a procession from each church walks through the town following a brass band. It meant a new frilly party dress and a posy of flowers.

I think we had flowers in our hair too. The streets were lined with onlookers and it was the custom if folk recognised you to give you money.

Coming from parents involved in family businesses with lots of customers and also having hundreds of Aunties, I did very well out of this. 'Remember you are walking for Jesus,' my sister said as I collected my drawstring money bag.

I looked at her blankly and nodded. The joy of the day was increased by an evening visit to the travelling fair in Bank Park. Here bright, kaleidoscopic patterned vans surrounded swings and stalls, all playing different music. It was a cacophony of sound, a riot of colour and tease of food smells.

My favourite aroma emanated from the doughnut machine – that sublime union of technology and culinary perfection. First a ring of white dough was squirted into a big bowl of hot, bubbling fat. The dough frizzled and joined a circular procession of doughnuts as they progressed from white to golden brown. Ejected, the doughnut was sprinkled with glistening white sugar and speared by the assistant onto a long metal prong. Genius.

I vowed I would have my own machine when I became a millionaire. As I grew into a teenager, the fair took on a different meaning. On the Waltzers, I noticed how the muscles of the fairground man bulged and rippled as he swung our carriage of laughing girls. The harder he swung it the more we screamed and all to the sound of Billy Fury singing 'Half Way to Paradise.' Indeed.

A Midsummer celebration might be:

- fresh baked whole salmon with summer salad
- strawberries, cream and optional meringues
- sparkling elderflower wine.

July 12th   End of term

Hurray! Hurrah! We sang with gusto, 'Lord dismiss us with thy blessing' and in the rush to escape school, we missed the poignancy of that line, 'All who here shall meet no more.' But who cared anyway? We didn't.

Yet today's school leavers are persuaded to care, persuaded of the importance of this occasion and persuaded to buy expensive clothes and hire Cadillacs in these newly styled American proms.

For children of the Fifties, the end of term heralded the annual week's holiday and for us, Uncle Ted's bungalow in Brown's Camp, Towyn, North Wales.

The bungalow was a converted tram with a double bedroom built on each end and the inner section made cosy with gas lamps, lace curtains, and a remaining pair of shiny black leather tram seats. The kitchenette was in the children's bedroom. I loved waking up to the smell of field mushrooms and bacon frying and Mum standing over it, such a change from Dad's daily porridge at home.

I'm in front of the happy holidays bungalow.

Towyn, 1950.

Birdsong floated in from the field through the top half opening of the barn-style door. The bungalow was heaven and if ever I have money to spare I would replicate it exactly but place it down the coast on the wild, western shore of Aberdaron, home of our children's family holidays.

There's a sacrifice involved in taking your children to camp in an empty field, empty except for kestrels, owls, grass snakes, butterflies and even a glow worm. There was no Happy Valley, the outdoor theatre of Llandudno, which my father loved.

Having been a band leader, he encouraged George and me to go on stage at the Happy Valley children's talent contest. 'George, you conduct the band. Jennifer you recite a poem.' I would follow my brother anywhere, even onto the stage where in the wings the other contestants waited.

From there I saw George conduct the band's playing of 'In the Mood', watched a girl sing 'The Good Ship Lollipop', a boy recite 'Albert and the Lion' and another boy play Grieg's piano concerto number one. He lifted his hands high in the air and crashed them down, hitting the right notes exactly from the top to the bottom of the piano. His funny expression meant George had to nudge me to stop my giggling.

Then I heard my name called. At eight years I knew no nerves. Dad had taught me 'Worth While' by Ella Wheeler Wilcox. I recited it without falter but I noticed my mother wiping a tear from her eye. This isn't going well I thought so I emphasised the last lines even though I had no idea what they meant,

> *'And the smile that is worth the praises of earth,*
> *is the smile that shines through tears.'*

The applause echoed through Happy Valley. Band leader and compere huddled to confer and after a roll on the drums I heard my name called again and somewhat puzzled, I was ushered forward to collect a five-shilling book token.

August 31ˢᵗ Blackberry season

The time blackberries ripen varies wildly from around the middle of August to the first week of September. For the next few weeks, elderberries, sloes, rosehips, haws, rowan berries, redcurrants, crab apples, wild pears, apples, plums, damsons, hazelnuts and mushrooms are ripe for the taking. Venture nowhere in autumn without a paper bag in a pocket. Look out too, for tables of surplus fruit and vegetables which appear outside people's houses with an honesty box for your money. This is nature's bounty.

Curiously, the blackberry is the only wild food that the English love collecting, perhaps because of its omnipresence in hedgerows and woods. Children of all ages love reaching out for the deep purple berries sitting in clusters in the sun, often tantalisingly out of reach but scratches are nothing for the primeval satisfaction of filling a basket with fruit for your pudding or pie.

Blackberry preparation:
Once home, lightly rinse in a sieve under the tap, place between kitchen paper and gently pat dry. Then you might eat them raw or freeze or cook them.

I tend to freezing because I am terrified of those little worms occasionally present and freezing kills them. Snakes, spiders, rats or headmasters I can handle but worms tend me to hysteria.

Anyway, place the washed, dried berries, not quite touching each other, on a rubber plate and 'open' freeze for an hour. Any worms present will surface in their battle for life and die, allowing me to flick them off. Pop into a zip poly bag and they will be 'free flow' so you can pour out what you need.

Blackberry recipes
Often blackberries can be extended or improved by the addition of some stewed apples. Likewise a few berries enhance apple puree but the ratio of one to the other is flexible. Stewed apples freeze superbly and with care can be sliced straight from the freezer. It's useful to have a bag of stewed apples in the freezer for quick desserts and for serving with roast pork as homemade apple sauce, so superior to the bland sloppy bought product.

Stewed blackberries

200g washed or frozen berries
1-2 tbsp sugar
1-2 tbsp water

Pop washed berries in a pan. Cover with a light sprinkling of sugar and add enough water to coat the bottom of the pan. (You need less water than you think as the heated fruit releases juice.) Simmer gently for a few minutes till softened.

Blackberry pies and puddings
Baking and sharing a pie is fun but if you are health conscious, you can do without the pastry. It is no sacrifice. If people were blindfolded and given a bowl of their chosen stewed fruit with their favourite topping of fresh cream, ice cream or custard and asked to rate the pleasure compared with a pie, I believe the result would show little difference.

But as we all like presenting and sharing a pie, consider making an open tart or use blackberries in summer puddings, trifles and syllabubs.

September Harvest Supper

Early in September most churches hold a harvest supper and my experience has ranged from:

- plated ham salad – still an old favourite with the English
- homemade hot pot followed by apple pie – this makes a lovely meal
- hot fish and chip supper prepared by the local chippy or pub

The supper is usually held in the village hall and may feature local musical talent. My husband and I even played at one. I was terrified not to have the support of the rest of our folk group but delighted to see Colonel Fitzhugh's walking stick beating time to my fiddle. Simple, intimate, communal village hall events where music or dancing or art exhibitions dominate are still a way of life with Celtic neighbours but not so much in England now.

Curiously, the tradition of decorating the church altar with seasonal fruit and vegetables is being replaced with food in tins, packets, jars and bottles which seems to miss the point of the seasonal celebration.

Stuart and I perform at the Frank Wingett fundraising appeal.
Overton-on-Dee, 1980.

31ˢᵗ October Halloween

'Thanks' again to the influence of our American cousins, Halloween is now more popular than Bonfire night and like the adoption of the American-style end-of-term proms, involves spending money on extravagant costumes.

But if you cannot beat it you might think of joining it. Once, I was forced to join in whilst having my five-year-old grandson, Lysander, to stay.

His brother had been admitted to hospital as an appendix emergency and I didn't want Lysander to be homesick or feel he was missing out on Halloween. Round the village we went at nightfall, he as Count Dracula and me as a witch. (No effort needed.)

The weather that night in Overton village was unusually balmy.

Everyone was friendly and little Lysander was impressed with the generosity of our neighbours: '*Oh he was a nice man wasn't he? Giving us all those sweets.*' I confess it was fun but not as much as Bonfire Night.

A simple Halloween supper

- bacon baps or burgers with bloody ketchup
- eyeball baps of halved boiled eggs with slices of gherkin or olives for pupils
- spaghetti worms
- dead fingers of moulded squashed figs with flaked almonds for nails
- spider web cake (or trifle) created by 'feather' icing. Pipe concentric circles, less than an inch apart and before it sets use a wet edged knife to lightly pull across the circle lines.
- chopped up green jelly covered in sweetie snakes.

Trick or treating with my grandson, Lysander.
October 2017.

Christmas Preparations for pudding and cake

The last week of October is a good time to make the Christmas pudding and cake as it coincides with half-term when enthusiastic little helpers are at home and perhaps you can demonstrate that it's better to make than to buy.

Homemade puddings always taste better so I have to remind myself to resist commercial hype about award-winning puddings. Making the pudding is easy as you just put everything in a big bowl, stir and make a wish. Collecting the long list of ingredients and placing them in the bowl ready to be weighed is the hardest part.

Some sources say Christmas pudding should be made in November on the last Sunday before Advent, 'Stir up' Sunday, they say. Whilst making the pudding on a Sunday allows each family member to stir and make a wish, I think it is a bit late. Wikipedia informs me that Advent is the period of build up before Christmas. I would call it tension and any preparations in advance should help to reduce this tension. A Christmas cake may take up to six months to mature, so making it early is a good idea. Once made, it needs to be fed brandy for weeks then marzipanned, dried out, flat iced, dried out and decorated and dried out again so starting this four to six week process early is essential. A quicker way is to let children rough up the royal icing like snow and add models of a snowman, robin, Santa, sleigh, Rudolph and so on before the icing sets. A full-time, working, harassed Mum might buy a plain fruit cake and let the children do this fun icing bit.

November 5th: Bonfire Night

Remember, remember the fifth of November!
Since Pagan times bonfires have been lit at this time of year and what a deeply satisfying ritual it is. A look into the white heat of the flames seems a look into all eternity: the past, the present and the future rolled into one. It is a deeply reflective experience and the haphazard flickering of the flames is beautiful and exciting, warming and comforting.

At bonfires past, there was no food or drink and no demand for it. Everything did not revolve around food and drink. We watched the bonfire start to die down, then lit a few simple fireworks, like Catherine wheels. Most exciting was the boys' throwing of penny bangers behind the girls whose screams of delight encouraged more. The finale was rockets flying over the Manchester Ship Canal and exploding in the sky. It was all over from start to finish in a couple of hours but the memory of communal fun never faded. And the fact that our bonfire was still smouldering the next day was a source of pride.

Simple food for a Bonfire Night Party

- hot soup served in mugs
- jacket potatoes baked in foil on the fire
- hotdogs or burgers on buns
- pitta bread stuffed with pilau rice
- parkin or gingerbread cake is traditional and has the merit of being tasty and easy to handle.

In the Fifties, Halloween was largely ignored but Bonfire Night never. Preparations started in early October by buying fireworks, one at a time, for a few pennies and storing them in a special tin. My tin, provided by my father, had Joshua Reynolds 'Age of Innocence' on the front.

Our fireworks were treasures, constantly examined, swopped and drooled over with fascinating names like Snow Storm, Emerald Mist, Rainbow Shower, Roman Candle, Moon Rocket, Mount Etna, Mount Vesuvius and so on.

Weeks before the big day, the building of the bonfire started in the backs with bonny wood collected by the bigger boys who sometimes dragged it home behind their bikes. Fears that a local teddy boy gang might steal our bonny wood caused look outs to be staged.

Anything less likely, I cannot imagine now but teddy boys then were the bogey men who were blamed for everything from Mrs Brown's heart attack, that broken window in the church or the disappearance of a pet cat.

The next stage was the making of a 'guy' by stuffing rolled up paper into your Dad's old clothes and adding a hat and a mask.

The guy was thrown into an old pram and pushed round the streets for approval and pennies. I had no idea who Guy Fawkes was.

Only later in life did I learn how he led a Catholic rebellion to blow up the Houses of Parliament. Having been tortured, he confessed and was sentenced to being hung, drawn and quartered.

On November 5th, school was an agony of waiting until the sky darkened and we were finally set free to run the mile home in minutes. At 6 o'clock the neighbours gathered in the backs of Greenbank Gardens and Dad lit the bonfire.

George Cruikshank's illustration of Guy Fawkes, published in William Harrison Ainsworth's 1840 novel Guy Fawkes.

Just the idea you were outside in the dark was exciting enough but the fire and fireworks were thrilling. It was weird talking in the dark to the familiar but disembodied voices of neighbours and very strange hearing your parents socialise in playful tones with other parents: a beginning of a realisation that Mum and Dad were also Esther and George and that they had other dimensions to their lives apart from us.

December: The Build-Up to Christmas

'Tis the season to be jolly'

Time to take to the woods with a basket and follow the Pagan tradition of bringing greenery into the home, a reminder that spring is on its way. Holly, snow berries and mistletoe make perfect Christmas floral arrangements.

Fresh flowers are expensive in December and central heating soon withers them but laurel and holly leaves will eke them out and leftovers can be kept fresh outside in a bucket of water.

Finally when you are in the mood and wish it could be Christmas every day, put up the decorations and let the fun begin.

Shopping can be a nightmare in December. If the big day ingredients are bought early, supermarket queues, jostling trolleys and fights over the last remaining selection box, all to the sound of *'So here it is, Merry Christmas, everybody's having fun,'* can be avoided along with hazardous driving conditions in fog or snow. Trimmings such as gravy, bread sauce and cranberry sauce may be made in advance and frozen.

Quality game and meat is available now and there are many vegetables to enjoy like Brussels sprouts, carrots, broccoli, cauliflower, celeriac, kale, parsnip, swede, spinach and turnip and salad vegetables. Ruby red cranberries, topaz clementines and ruddy brown chestnuts are at their seasonal best too.

With such colourful food sold alongside the holly and mistletoe and the glimpse of turkeys hanging in the back, no wonder Dad said there was no need to decorate the shop at Christmas. It did it itself.

I try to stock up on preserved treats such as peaches in brandy or plums in Madeira for quick desserts. In the first week of December the Christmas cake can be almond pasted, in the second week flat iced which allows time to decorate in the third week.

If unexpected guests arrive in the middle of all this, try:

A simple seasonal meal:

- **sausage casserole**
- **mashed potato**
- **red cabbage and sprouts**
- **syllabub**

All these dishes are quickly whipped up. Like mince pies and mulled wine, syllabub is mediaeval in origin and provides a satisfying link to the past, as well as tasting good.

The Christmas dinner is easier if the load is shared. Some extended families arrange a hot buffet meal where each family or person provides an item. I once cooked the Christmas turkey and transported it fifty miles to mother-in-law's in an insulated box with the trimmings and she did the vegetables. It worked brilliantly.

Sometimes it suits to eat the meal out, perhaps on Christmas Eve, when the price hasn't doubled, so everyone can be relaxed on Christmas Day. Quite rightly, we worry about the old being lonely at Christmas but in my experience many 'older' folk are sometimes glad of the peace and quiet.

A friend of mine once steadfastly refused family invitations to Christmas lunch and took a picnic basket to the seaside where she happily dined on the beach, alone.

Christmas Times past

For many of us, though, the urge to recreate our childhood Christmas is irresistible. In the Fifties, my childhood Christmas was a hectic time for Mum and Dad.

All of Mum's hairdressing customers wanted to look good for Christmas and Dad was run off his feet organising Hill and

Glover's sale of Christmas trees, holly and mistletoe on top of groceries and green groceries, flowers for funerals and weddings and the hanging and drawing turkeys.

On Christmas Eve, Mum would have preferred that Dad did not join his brothers in a brass band concert of carols given when the 'closed' sign finally went up in the shop. 'Never marry into a family business,' she would tell me but the family parties that followed were great.

Uncle Jim, Uncle Tom, my father and grandfather
of Latchford Silver Band. Warrington, circa 1930.

Retro 1950s Buffet

- pork pies
- sausages on sticks
- celery sticks in a jug
- cheese and pineapple on sticks
- vol-au-vents stuffed with mushroom or prawn sauce
- open finger rolls topped with ham or egg and salad cream

My Aunty Peggy and Uncle Jim hosted big parties for Hill & Glover, High Class Fruiterers & Florists, as well as family Christmas parties. Their house was a big semi-detached in posh suburbia with those fascinating bells in the kitchen where previous occupants would ring for their servants. The grown-ups collected in the drawing room where the aunties kissed you and commented on how bigger and older you were getting. Then I would join my cousins in the living room where they played Bill Haley, Cliff Richard or Elvis on the record player and danced and generally showed how cool they were.

After a while it was obvious from the laughs next door that the oldies were having more fun so it was only a matter of time before the youngsters migrated and the record player was silent. Live music triumphed as it always does. First Uncle Stan and Aunty Maggie sang, 'I'll take you home Kathleen' the words of which powerfully stirred my imagination.

Whatever was wrong with Kathleen? I was also deeply impressed by a husband and wife singing in harmony. Then there was the family brass band, composed of uncles and cousins.

Uncle Stan, accompanied by Barbara Ball. Those Glover parties were amazing and still talked about today.

The Large Room, Grappenhall, 1959.

The brass ensemble was preceded by much chatter, tuning of instruments, puffing and the final positioning of instruments before a respectful expectant hush descended.

My Uncle Jim gave the nod and counted one, two, three and, as if by magic, these big bulky instruments blended into one pure harmonious sound. 'Mary's Boy Child' started, 'Silent Night' might follow and 'Jingle Bells' might end the concert. In between

were all sorts of acts and funny repartee, particularly from Aunty
Peggy who, unfazed at not playing an instrument, would dance
about playing a tin tray like a tambourine, her beautiful gypsy eyes
blazing and making everyone laugh with her witty quips.

But she was always respectfully quiet when the musicians were
playing. I took it all for granted that everybody had family parties
like this and only much later in life did I realise how blessed I was.

Uncle Jim leads the conga which signalled: the party's over.

APPENDIX

FOOD DICTIONARY

Agave nectar is one of the most popular sugar substitutes. It looks like honey and tastes good. It has a low glycaemic index which you might think made it healthier. But nothing is straightforward and some experts argue that it could be less healthy in the long run.

Arborio is an Italian short grain rice used in puddings, risottos and sushi. Basmati rice from India is a longer grain and a little more flavoursome. It is most commonly used in curries and savoury dishes. Jasmine rice from Thailand has long slender grains too but becomes sticky when cooked. Wash all rice well before use.

Ayurvedic is ancient Hindu healing through diet and yoga.

Baking paper or parchment is silicone coated and dearer than greaseproof. Good for lining simple tins. It requires no greasing and the shiny side should touch the food.

Cacao: a purer, less processed chocolate powder than cocoa with the likelihood of more anti-oxidants and magnesium.

Cocoa: a cheaper, heat processed form of chocolate powder and still very healthy if bought without added sugar. (Drinking chocolate has added sugar.) It can be used instead of cacao, the purer and slightly healthier version of chocolate powder.

Homemade and home-baked: some shops' use of these terms may be misleading. Homemade suggests pure, fresh ingredients. Bakeries often say their bread is home baked but it may be made of processed imported ingredients reconstituted by the baker with water and not a simple homemade product at all. Buyer beware.

Lucoma: not a brain disease but a Peruvian super fruit available as a super food in powder form. It is considered by some to be a healthier sweetener than sugar.

Maca: Peruvian herb available in powder form. It has a malty taste and is usually added to smoothies, puddings, juices and raw sweets. All manner of health claims are made for it. I tried it in cakes but didn't like it.

Pancetta: Italian bacon from pork belly that is salt cured and lightly spiced. It is raw like our bacon.

Prosciutto: means ham. Parma ham is prosciutto from Parma!

Polenta: Italian corn meal

Sumac: fruit powder with a lemon tangy taste. It is used in Middle Eastern cooking instead of lemon for salads and grilled meat or fish. It is supposed to be an antioxidant and is available from Amazon at a price.

Tamarind: pod of reddish-black fruit. It tastes sweet and tangy but earthy. Used in curries and chutneys; its strong flavour means only a little is needed.

Tisane is a herbal infusion enjoyed for its taste and health benefits.

Waxed lemons have a coating of wax to preserve them in transit. For zesting and grating unwaxed seems preferable.

Xanthan gum: is used to thicken sauces, dressings and purees, mainly by processors. When I first read it on an ingredients label, I thought it sounded like a nasty chemical additive but far from it. It is a fermented sugar and harmless, possibly even beneficial in small amounts. It is certainly useful and quick to use when foods need to be bound together smoothly.

Xylitol: a natural replacement for cane sugar which some dentists recommend as it is less likely to cause tooth decay. It looks like sugar and is supposed to be interchangeable but I thought I detected a slight after taste. Stevia is another sugar substitute. Obviously weaning yourself off sweet food is the healthiest idea.

USEFUL WEIGHTS & MEASURES

Most kitchen measures are approximate. Weighing is more accurate.

Measuring spoons

1 tsp (teaspoon)	= 5ml
4 tsp	= 1 tbsp (tablespoon)
1 tbsp	= 20ml

Spoon measurements are level. If the recipe says use a rounded spoon that equals two level spoons of the same.

Flour	2 level tbsp	= 25g (1oz)
Sugar	2 level tbsp	= 25g (1oz)
Rice	2 level tbsp	= 25g (1oz)
Currants etc	2 level tbsp	= 25g (1oz)
Syrup, treacle	1 level tbsp	= 25g (1oz)

American measuring cups

The American cuisine is varied and probably under estimated in the UK. When using American recipes, an American cup is needed for measuring.

On a journey from Atlanta to New Orleans, I looked for a set of cups at every big store near where the coach stopped but to no avail. Finally, in a beautiful hardware shop in a corner of New Orleans I found them.

1 cup flour	= 125g (4oz)
1 cup sugar	= 225g (8oz)
1 cup icing sugar	= 125g (4oz)
1 cup raw rice	= 200g (7oz)
1 cup grated cheese	= 125g (4oz)
1 cup dried fruit	= 150g (5oz)
1 cup liquid	= 250ml (8 fl oz)

Metric and Imperial

1oz	= 28.3g (usually converted to 25g for ease of arithmetic).
1 kg	= 2lb 3oz
1 litre	= 1¾ pint, 35 fluid ounces
1 pint	= 20 fluid ounces (568ml ie. 600ml)
½ pint	= 10 fluid ounces (284ml ie. 300ml)

Oven Temperatures

Very hot	240-250°C	bread
Hot	220-230°C	rich yeast mixtures, Yorkshire pud
Moderately hot	190-200°C	roast meat, pastries
Moderate	170-180°C	cakes and biscuits
Moderately cool	150-170°C	fruit cakes, stews
Cool	130-140°C	some puddings
Very cool	100-120°C	meringues

Fan-assisted ovens cook faster. Reduce temperature according to manufacturer's guidance.

Raising Agents: plain flour and baking powder and yeast

Self-raising flour is suitable for cakes and biscuits as it has a relatively small proportion of soft gluten. Its raising power equals 4 level tsp per pound (450g) of baking powder making it only suitable for scones and plain cakes – some benefit from a little extra baking powder:
2½-3 level tsp of baking powder to ½ lb (200g) plain flour suits scones so if using SR flour a little extra BP might be added.
1½ tsp to ½ lb (200g) plain flour for sandwich cakes or fairy cakes so SR flour is usually all right. With yeast, 1tsp of dried yeast is equivalent to 11g of fresh yeast.

TIPS ON SAUCE AND PASTRY MAKING

SAUCE MAKING

White sauce is the basis of many savoury dishes. It requires a short period of intense concentration and patience. Plenty of stirring and the slow addition of liquid and heat helps to avoid lumps. If you rush and lumps appear an electric whisk will usually remove them.

White sauces may be made as a:

Pouring sauce: The proportions are 19g (¾ oz) butter or margarine, 19g (¾ oz) flour, 250ml milk (½ pint).

Coating sauce: This is the most commonly used sauce. The proportions are 25g (1oz) margarine or butter, 25g (1oz) flour, 250ml (½ pint) milk or milk with liquor and seasoning.

The old method of making is to melt the fat and add the flour to make the roux (small ball). Cook 2 minutes. Slowly stir in liquid and gradually bring to the boil stirring all the time for a good minute.

The all-in-one method may also be used: margarine or butter is placed in pan with flour and milk and a lot of frantic stirring is done as it is gradually brought to boiling point.

Flavourings of white sauces include mustard, mushroom, onion, parsley and most commonly cheese. Cheese should be stirred in grated whilst sauce is still warm but not boiling.

Brown Sauce
This is a most useful skill as a brown sauce is often the basis of savoury dishes like stews and casseroles.

Nearly all stews start with frying onions. Then other vegetables may be sautéed or 'fat steamed' alongside. Flour may be added now to make a 'roux'. A roux is an equal mix of fat and flour which forms a ball and is cooked for 1-2 minutes. It smoothly thickens the liquid when added gradually and brought to boiling point. If wine or anything acidic like tomatoes is added next, this liquor is less likely to become lumpy.

PASTRY

Short or shortcrust is the most commonly-used pastry. The basic proportions are half fat to flour.

Eg: 100g fat is rubbed into 220g flour until it looks like fine bread-crumbs. Water is slowly added till it looks like big pieces which can be drawn together by hand into one big ball. Relax the pastry in the fridge if possible before rolling out.

Sprinkle rolling pin and table top lightly with flour and roll lightly with many turns of the rolling pin. Avoid heavy handed bashing into the table. Firm but gentle is the rule. Bake at 200°C for 20 minutes.

Suet pastry
This is the easiest pastry to make. Again it uses half fat (suet) to flour (SR flour.) Simply, scatter shredded suet onto flour already weighed in a bowl. Gently stir in water till big lumps are formed which can be drawn together into a ball by hand. Roll lightly as directed above till ¼-inch thick.

This pastry makes a good pie crust and is baked for 20 minutes at 200°C. It may be used for jam roly-poly and can be boiled in stews for dumplings. Best of all it is steamed or microwaved for steak and kidney pudding or dessert puddings.

Index

Printed in Great Britain
by Amazon

52744744R00129